Documentary Film: A Very Short Introduction

VERY SHORT INTRODUCTIONS are for anyone wanting a stimulating and accessible way in to a new subject. They are written by experts, and have been published in more than twenty-five languages worldwide.

The series began in 1995 and now represents a wide variety of topics in history, philosophy, religion, science, and the humanities. Over the next few years it will grow to a library of around 200 volumes—a Very Short Introduction to everything from ancient Egypt and Indian philosophy to conceptual art and cosmology.

Very Short Introductions available now:

AFRICAN HISTORY John Parker and Richard Rathbone
AMERICAN POLITICAL PARTIES AND ELECTIONS L. Sandy Maisel
THE AMERICAN PRESIDENCY Charles O. Jones
ANARCHISM Colin Ward
ANCIENT EGYPT Ian Shaw
ANCIENT PHILOSOPHY Julia Annas
ANCIENT WARFARE Harry Sidebottom
ANGLICANISM Mark Chapman
THE ANGLO-SAXON AGE John Blair
ANIMAL RIGHTS David DeGrazia
ANTISEMITISM Steven Beller
ARCHAEOLOGY Paul Bahn
ARCHITECTURE Andrew Ballantyne
ARISTOTLE Jonathan Barnes
ART HISTORY Dana Arnold
ART THEORY Cynthia Freeland
THE HISTORY OF ASTRONOMY Michael Hoskin
ATHEISM Julian Baggini
AUGUSTINE Henry Chadwick
BARTHES Jonathan Culler
BESTSELLERS John Sutherland
THE BIBLE John Riches
THE BRAIN Michael O'Shea
BRITISH POLITICS Anthony Wright
BUDDHA Michael Carrithers
BUDDHISM Damien Keown
BUDDHIST ETHICS Damien Keown
CAPITALISM James Fulcher
THE CELTS Barry Cunliffe
CHAOS Leonard Smith

CHOICE THEORY Michael Allingham
CHRISTIAN ART Beth Williamson
CHRISTIANITY Linda Woodhead
CLASSICS Mary Beard and John Henderson
CLASSICAL MYTHOLOGY Helen Morales
CLAUSEWITZ Michael Howard
THE COLD WAR Robert McMahon
CONSCIOUSNESS Susan Blackmore
CONTEMPORARY ART Julian Stallabrass
CONTINENTAL PHILOSOPHY Simon Critchley
COSMOLOGY Peter Coles
THE CRUSADES Christopher Tyerman
CRYPTOGRAPHY Fred Piper and Sean Murphy
DADA AND SURREALISM David Hopkins
DARWIN Jonathan Howard
THE DEAD SEA SCROLLS Timothy Lim
DEMOCRACY Bernard Crick
DESCARTES Tom Sorell
DESIGN John Heskett
DINOSAURS David Norman
DOCUMENTARY FILM Patricia Aufderheide
DREAMING J. Allan Hobson
DRUGS Leslie Iversen
THE EARTH Martin Redfern
ECONOMICS Partha Dasgupta
EGYPTIAN MYTH Geraldine Pinch
EIGHTEENTH-CENTURY BRITAIN Paul Langford

THE ELEMENTS Philip Ball
EMOTION Dylan Evans
EMPIRE Stephen Howe
ENGELS Terrell Carver
ETHICS Simon Blackburn
THE EUROPEAN UNION John Pinder
EVOLUTION Brian and
    Deborah Charlesworth
EXISTENTIALISM Thomas Flynn
FASCISM Kevin Passmore
FEMINISM Margaret Walters
THE FIRST WORLD WAR
    Michael Howard
FOSSILS Keith Thomson
FOUCAULT Gary Gutting
THE FRENCH REVOLUTION
    William Doyle
FREE WILL Thomas Pink
FREUD Anthony Storr
FUNDAMENTALISM Malise Ruthven
GALILEO Stillman Drake
GAME THEORY Ken Binmore
GANDHI Bhikhu Parekh
GEOPOLITICS Klaus Dodds
GLOBAL CATASTROPHES Bill McGuire
GLOBALIZATION Manfred Steger
GLOBAL WARMING Mark Maslin
THE GREAT DEPRESSION AND THE
    NEW DEAL Eric Rauchway
HABERMAS James Gordon Finlayson
HEGEL Peter Singer
HEIDEGGER Michael Inwood
HIEROGLYPHS Penelope Wilson
HINDUISM Kim Knott
HISTORY John H. Arnold
HOBBES Richard Tuck
HUMAN EVOLUTION Bernard Wood
HUMAN RIGHTS Andrew Clapham
HUME A. J. Ayer
IDEOLOGY Michael Freeden
INDIAN PHILOSOPHY Sue Hamilton
INTELLIGENCE Ian J. Deary
INTERNATIONAL
    MIGRATION Khalid Koser
INTERNATIONAL RELATIONS
    Paul Wilkinson
ISLAM Malise Ruthven
JOURNALISM Ian Hargreaves
JUDAISM Norman Solomon
JUNG Anthony Stevens

KABBALAH Joseph Dan
KAFKA Ritchie Robertson
KANT Roger Scruton
KIERKEGAARD Patrick Gardiner
THE KORAN Michael Cook
LINGUISTICS Peter Matthews
LITERARY THEORY Jonathan Culler
LOCKE John Dunn
LOGIC Graham Priest
MACHIAVELLI Quentin Skinner
THE MARQUIS DE SADE John Phillips
MARX Peter Singer
MATHEMATICS Timothy Gowers
MEDICAL ETHICS Tony Hope
MEDIEVAL BRITAIN John Gillingham
    and Ralph A. Griffiths
MODERN ART David Cottington
MODERN IRELAND Senia Pašeta
MOLECULES Philip Ball
MUSIC Nicholas Cook
MYTH Robert A. Segal
NATIONALISM Steven Grosby
THE NEW TESTAMENT AS
    LITERATURE Kyle Keefer
NEWTON Robert Iliffe
NIETZSCHE Michael Tanner
NINETEENTH-CENTURY
    BRITAIN Christopher Harvie and
    H. C. G. Matthew
NORTHERN IRELAND
    Marc Mulholland
PARTICLE PHYSICS Frank Close
PAUL E. P. Sanders
PHILOSOPHY Edward Craig
PHILOSOPHY OF LAW
    Raymond Wacks
PHILOSOPHY OF SCIENCE
    Samir Okasha
PHOTOGRAPHY Steve Edwards
PLATO Julia Annas
POLITICS Kenneth Minogue
POLITICAL PHILOSOPHY
    David Miller
POSTCOLONIALISM Robert Young
POSTMODERNISM Christopher Butler
POSTSTRUCTURALISM
    Catherine Belsey
PREHISTORY Chris Gosden
PRESOCRATIC
    PHILOSOPHY Catherine Osborne

PSYCHOLOGY Gillian Butler and Freda McManus
PSYCHIATRY Tom Burns
QUANTUM THEORY John Polkinghorne
RACISM Ali Rattansi
THE RENAISSANCE Jerry Brotton
RENAISSANCE ART Geraldine A. Johnson
ROMAN BRITAIN Peter Salway
THE ROMAN EMPIRE Christopher Kelly
ROUSSEAU Robert Wokler
RUSSELL A. C. Grayling
RUSSIAN LITERATURE Catriona Kelly
THE RUSSIAN REVOLUTION S. A. Smith
SCHIZOPHRENIA Chris Frith and Eve Johnstone
SCHOPENHAUER Christopher Janaway
SHAKESPEARE Germaine Greer
SIKHISM Eleanor Nesbitt
SOCIAL AND CULTURAL ANTHROPOLOGY John Monaghan and Peter Just
SOCIALISM Michael Newman
SOCIOLOGY Steve Bruce
SOCRATES C. C. W. Taylor
THE SPANISH CIVIL WAR Helen Graham
SPINOZA Roger Scruton
STUART BRITAIN John Morrill
TERRORISM Charles Townshend
THEOLOGY David F. Ford
THE HISTORY OF TIME Leofranc Holford-Strevens
TRAGEDY Adrian Poole
THE TUDORS John Guy
TWENTIETH-CENTURY BRITAIN Kenneth O. Morgan
THE VIKINGS Julian Richards
WITTGENSTEIN A. C. Grayling
WORLD MUSIC Philip Bohlman
THE WORLD TRADE ORGANIZATION Amrita Narlikar

Available soon:

EXPRESSIONISM Katerina Reed-Tsocha
GEOGRAPHY John Matthews and David Herbert
GERMAN LITERATURE Nicholas Boyle
HIV/AIDS Alan Whiteside
MEMORY Jonathan Foster
MODERN CHINA Rana Mitter
QUAKERISM Pink Dandelion
SCIENCE AND RELIGION Thomas Dixon
SEXUALITY Veronique Mottier

For more information visit our website

www.oup.co.uk/general/vsi/

Patricia Aufderheide

DOCUMENTARY FILM

A Very Short Introduction

OXFORD
UNIVERSITY PRESS

OXFORD
UNIVERSITY PRESS

Oxford University Press, Inc., publishes works that further
Oxford University's objective of excellence
in research, scholarship, and education.

Oxford New York
Auckland Cape Town Dar es Salaam Hong Kong Karachi
Kuala Lumpur Madrid Melbourne Mexico City Nairobi
New Delhi Shanghai Taipei Toronto

With offices in
Argentina Austria Brazil Chile Czech Republic France Greece
Guatemala Hungary Italy Japan Poland Portugal Singapore
South Korea Switzerland Thailand Turkey Ukraine Vietnam

Copyright © 2007 by Patricia Aufderheide

Published by Oxford University Press, Inc.
198 Madison Avenue, New York, NY 10016

www.oup.com

Oxford is a registered trademark of Oxford University Press

All rights reserved. No part of this publication may be reproduced,
stored in a retrieval system, or transmitted, in any form or by any means,
electronic, mechanical, photocopying, recording, or otherwise,
without the prior permission of Oxford University Press.

Library of Congress Cataloging-in-Publication Data
Aufderheide, Patricia.
Documentary film : a very short introduction
/ Patricia Aufderheide.
p. cm.—(Very short introductions)
Includes bibliographical references and index.
ISBN 978-0-19-518270-5 (pbk.)
1. Documentary films—History and criticism.
I. Title.
PN1995.9.D6A94 2007
070.1'8—dc22
2007018114

7 9 8

Printed in Great Britain
by Ashford Colour Press Ltd., Gosport, Hants.
on acid-free paper

Contents

List of Illustrations viii

Introduction ix

1 Defining the documentary 1
   Naming 1
   Form 10
   Founders 25
   Cinema verité 44

2 Subgenres 56
   Public affairs 56
   Government propaganda 65
   Advocacy 77
   Historical 91
   Ethnographic 106
   Nature 117

3 Conclusion 125
   A note on history and scholarship 128

   One Hundred Great Documentaries 137

   Further Reading and Viewing 140

   Index 147

List of Illustrations

1 Toxic effects of vinyl production explored in *Blue Vinyl*.   8
© Chris Pilaro

2 Moth wings and scraps of twigs and flowers in *Mothlight*.   17
Estate of Stan Brakhage and www.fredcamper.com

3 Traditional Inuit customs in *Nanook of the North*.   29
Library of Congress

4 British mailtrain in *Night Mail*.   34
Museum of Modern Art Film Stills Archive

5 Camera lens in *Man with a Movie Camera*.   43
© Photofest

6 Seller of Bibles in *Salesman*.   48
© Photofest

7 African American basketball player in *Hoop Dreams*.   54
© Kartemquin Films 1994

8 Crowd scene from *Triumph of the Will*.   72
© Photofest

9 Transatlantic phone call in *The New Americans*.   89
© Kartemquin Films 2004

10 Armored tanks as shown in *The Battle of Chile*.   103
First Run/Icarus Films

11 Bodyguards of Salvador Allende, in *Chile, Obstinate memory*.   103
First Run/Icarus Films

12 Amazonian Indians in *The Smell of the Pequi Fruit*.   115
Video in the Villages

13 Al Gore presents *An Inconvenient Truth*.   123
© 2006 by Paramount Classics, a division of Paramount Pictures

Introduction

This introduction to documentary film is directed to people who like watching documentaries and want to know more about the form; to people who hope to make documentaries and want to know the field and its expectations; and to students and teachers who hope to learn more and tell others what they have learned.

Documentary Film is organized to present an overview of central issues and then to discuss different subgenres. I particularly wanted to use categories that could address concerns about objectivity, advocacy, and bias that have always swirled around documentary but with renewed vigor since the breakthrough popularity of *Fahrenheit 9/11*. One could easily select or add other categories, such as music, sports, labor, diary, and food; I selected the ones used in this book because they are common categories in the documentary marketplace, and because they raise important issues about truth and representing reality.

This thematic organization allows you to enter the subject matter easily through the kind of film that first attracted you to it, and it allows me to make connections between historical eras and to demonstrate the ongoing nature of core controversies in documentary. Those who prefer a more straightforward chronology may note that each of the subgenre chapters is organized chronologically (with the exception of the propaganda chapter, which focuses largely on World War II). So after reading the first four chapters, which establish the core issues and early documentary history, one can read the first sections of the various subgenre chapters and then return to the next section of each of the chapters.

Since the material is drawn not only from scholarship but from my four-decade experience as a film critic, it reflects my interests and limitations. Most of the scholarship I refer to is written in English, and I have a bias toward long-form documentary and the work of independent filmmakers.

I was originally attracted to documentary by the promise that has drawn so many makers to the form—one that the noted editor and critic Dai Vaughan, in an essay concerned with the threat to documentary by digital manipulation, described as the "gut feeling that if people were allowed to see freely they would see truly, perceiving their world as open to scrutiny and evaluation, as being malleable in the way film is malleable." I have found the work of filmmakers such as Les Blank, Henry Hampton, Pirjo Honkasalo, Barbara Kopple, Kim Longinotto, Marcel Ophuls, Gordon Quinn, and Agnès Varda to be inspiring.

I am grateful to Elda Rotor of the Oxford University Press for approaching me with the idea of writing this book, and to Cybele Tom for shouldering the editing upon her departure, and to my copy editor, Mary Sutherland. Many colleagues in communication, literature, film, and film studies programs generously provided insights that I attempt to share here. I greatly appreciate the support of American University's library staff, especially Chris Lewis. I am indebted to Ron Sutton, my mentor at American University; to Dean Larry Kirkman at the American University School of Communication, who also did me the inestimable honor of introducing me to Erik Barnouw; and to New York University's Barbara Abrash, who opened many doors to insight and opportunity. Projects with the Council on Foundations (especially with Evelyn Gibson) and the Ford Foundation (especially with Orlando Bagwell) deepened my knowledge of the field. I am grateful as well to Gordon Quinn, Nina Seavey, Stephan Schwartzman, George Stoney, and anonymous reviewers for comments in production.

Chapter 1
Defining the Documentary

Naming

Documentary film begins in the last years of the nineteenth century with the first films ever projected, and it has many faces. It can be a trip to exotic lands and lifestyles, as was *Nanook of the North* (1922). It can be a visual poem, such as Joris Ivens's *Rain* (1929)—a story about a rainy day, set to a piece of classical music, in which the storm echoes the structure of the music. It can be an artful piece of propaganda. Soviet filmmaker Dziga Vertov, who ardently proclaimed that fiction cinema was poisonous and dying and that documentary was the future, made *Man with a Movie Camera* (1929) as propaganda both for a political regime and for a film style.

What is a documentary? One easy and traditional answer is: not a movie. Or at least not a movie like *Star Wars* is a movie. Except when it *is* a theatrical movie, like *Fahrenheit 9/11* (2004), which broke all box-office records for a documentary. Another easy and common answer could be: a movie that isn't fun, a serious movie, something that tries to teach you something—except when it's something like Stacy Peralta's *Riding Giants* (2004), which gives you a thrill ride on the history of surfing. Many documentaries are cannily designed with the express goal of entertainment. Indeed, most documentary filmmakers consider themselves storytellers, not journalists.

A simple answer might be: a movie about real life. And that is precisely the problem; documentaries are *about* real life; they are not real life. They are not even windows onto real life. They are portraits of real life, using real life as their raw material, constructed by artists and technicians who make myriad decisions about what story to tell to whom, and for what purpose.

You might then say: a movie that does its best to represent real life and that doesn't manipulate it. And yet, there is no way to make a film without manipulating the information. Selection of topic, editing, mixing sound are all manipulations. Broadcast journalist Edward R. Murrow once said, "Anyone who believes that every individual film must represent a 'balanced' picture knows nothing about either balance or pictures."

The problem of deciding how much to manipulate is as old as the form. *Nanook of the North* is considered one of the first great documentaries, but its subjects, the Inuit, assumed roles at filmmaker Robert Flaherty's direction, much like actors in a fiction film. Flaherty asked them to do things they no longer did, such as hunt for walrus with a spear, and he showed them as ignorant about things they understood. In the film, "Nanook"—not his real name—bites a gramophone record in cheerful puzzlement, but in fact the man was quite savvy about modern equipment and even helped Flaherty disassemble and reassemble his camera equipment regularly. At the same time, Flaherty built his story from his own experience of years living with the Inuit, who happily participated in his project and gave him plenty of ideas for the plot.

A documentary film tells a story about real life, with claims to truthfulness. How to do that honestly, in good faith, is a never-ending discussion, with many answers. Documentary is defined and redefined over the course of time, both by makers and by viewers. Viewers certainly shape the meaning of any documentary, by combining our own knowledge of and interest in the world with how the filmmaker shows it to us. Audience expectations are also built on prior experience; viewers expect not to be tricked and lied to. We expect to be told things about the real world, things that are true.

We do not demand that these things be portrayed objectively, and they do not have to be the complete truth. The filmmaker may employ poetic license from time to time and refer to reality symbolically (an image of the Colosseum representing, say, a European vacation). But we do expect that a documentary will be a fair and honest representation of somebody's experience of reality. This is the contract with the viewer that teacher Michael Rabiger meant in his classic text: "There are no rules in this young art form, only decisions about where to draw the line and how to remain consistent to the contract you will set up with your audience."

Terms

The term "documentary" emerged awkwardly out of early practice. When entrepreneurs in the late nineteenth century first began to record moving pictures of real-life events, some called what they were making "documentaries." The term did not stabilize for decades, however. Other people called their films "educationals," "actualities," "interest films," or perhaps referred to their subject matter—"travel films," for example. John Grierson, a Scot, decided to use this new form in the service of the British government and coined the term "documentary" by applying it to the work of the great American filmmaker Robert Flaherty's *Moana* (1926), which chronicled daily life on a South Seas island. He defined documentary as the "artistic representation of actuality"—a definition that has proven durable probably because it is so very flexible.

Marketing pressures affect what is defined as a documentary. When the philosopher-filmmaker Errol Morris's *The Thin Blue Line* (1988) was released in theaters, public relations professionals downplayed the term "documentary" in the interest of ticket sales. The film is a sophisticated detective story—did Randall Adams commit the crime for which he is sentenced to die in Texas? The film shows the dubious quality of key witnesses' testimony. When the case was reopened and the film entered as evidence, the film's status suddenly became important, and Morris now had to assert that it was, indeed, a documentary.

Conversely, Michael Moore's first feature, *Roger and Me* (1989), a savage indictment of General Motors for precipitating the decline of the steel town of Flint, Michigan, and a masterpiece of black humor, was originally called a documentary. But when journalist Harlan Jacobson showed that Moore had misrepresented the sequence of events, Moore distanced himself from the word "documentary." He argued that this was not a documentary but a movie, an entertainment whose deviations from strict sequencing were incidental to the theme.

In the 1990s, documentaries began to be big business worldwide, and by 2004 the worldwide business in television documentary alone added up to $4.5 billion revenues annually. Reality TV and "docusoaps"—real-life miniseries set in potentially high-drama situations such as driving schools, restaurants, hospitals, and airports—also burgeoned. Theatrical revenues multiplied at the beginning of the twenty-first century. DVD sales, video-on-demand, and rentals of documentaries became big business. Soon documentaries were being made for cell phones, and collaborative documentaries were being produced online. Marketers who had discreetly hidden the fact that their films were documentaries were now proudly calling such works "docs."

Why it matters

Naming matters. Names come with expectations; if that were not true, then marketers would not use them as marketing tools. The truthfulness, accuracy, and trustworthiness of documentaries are important to us all because we value them precisely and uniquely for these qualities. When documentarians deceive us, they are not just deceiving viewers but members of the public who might act upon knowledge gleaned from the film. Documentaries are part of the media that help us understand not only our world but our role in it, that shape us as public actors.

The importance of documentaries is thus linked to a notion of the public as a social phenomenon. The philosopher John Dewey argued persuasively that the public—the body so crucial to the health of a democratic society—is not just individuals added up. A public is a group of people who can act together for the public good and so can hold to account the entrenched power of business and government. It is an informal body that can come together in crisis if need be. There are as many publics as there are occasions and issues to call them forth. We can all be members of any particular public, if we have a way to communicate with each other about the shared problems we face. Communication, therefore, is the soul of the public.

As communications scholar James Carey noted, "Reality is a scarce resource." Reality is not *what* is out there but what we *know*, *understand*, and *share* with each other of what is out there. Media affect the most expensive real estate of all, that which is inside your head. Documentary is an important reality-shaping communication, because of its claims to truth. Documentaries are always grounded in real life, and make a claim to tell us something worth knowing about it.

True, consumer entertainment is an important aspect of the business of filmmaking, even in documentary. Most documentary filmmakers sell their work, either to viewers or to intermediaries such as broadcasters and distributors. They are constrained by their business models. Even though documentary costs much less than fiction film to make, it is still much more expensive to produce than, say, a brochure or a pamphlet. Television and theatrical documentaries usually require investors or institutions such as broadcasters to back them. And as documentaries become ever more popular, more of them are being produced to delight audiences without challenging assumptions. They attract and distract with the best-working tools, including sensationalism, sex, and violence. Theatrical wildlife films such as *March of the Penguins* (2005) are classic examples of consumer entertainment that use all of these techniques to charm and alarm viewers, even though the sensationalism, sex, and violence occur among animals.

Paid persuaders also exploit the reality claims of the genre, often as operatives of government and business. This may produce devastating social results, as did Nazi propaganda such as the viciously anti-Semitic *The Eternal Jew* (1937). Such work may also provoke important positive change. When the Roosevelt administration wanted to sell Americans on expensive new government programs, it commissioned some of the most remarkable visual poems made in the era, those by Pare Lorentz and a talented team. Works such as *The Plow that Broke the Plains* (1936) and *The River* (1938) helped to invest taxpayers in programs that promoted economic stability and growth.

In its short history, however, documentary has often been made by individuals on the edges of mainstream media, working with a public service media organization such as public broadcasting, with commercial broadcasters eager for awards, with nonprofit entities, or with private foundation or public education funds. On the margins of mainstream media, slightly off-kilter from status-quo understandings of reality, many documentarians have struggled to speak truthfully about—and to—power. They have often seen themselves as public actors, speaking not only to audiences but to other members of a public that needs to know in order to act.

Some recent examples demonstrate the range of such activity. Brave New Films's *Wal-Mart: The High Cost of Low Price* (2005) is an impassioned, didactic argument indicting the large retail superstore for such practices as inadequate medical plans for employees and the willful destruction of small businesses. It does not strive for balance in representing Wal-Mart's point of view; it does strive for accuracy in representing the problem. The film was made for action; it was used to organize legislative pushback and social resistance to the company's most exploitative practices. Wal-Mart aggressively countered the film with attack ads, and the filmmakers countercharged Wal-Mart with inaccuracy. Bloggers and even mainstream media picked up the discussion. Brave New Films positioned itself as a voice of the public, filling a perceived gap in the coverage that mainstream media provided on the problem. Viewers of the film, most of whom saw it through DVD-by-mail purchases and as a result of an e-mail campaign, viewed it not as entertainment but as an entertainingly-produced argument about an important public issue.

Michael Moore's *Fahrenheit 9/11*, a sardonic, anti-Iraq war film, addressed the American public directly, as people whose government was acting in the public's name. Right-wing commentators in commercial media attempted to discredit the film by charging that it was indeed propaganda. But Moore is not a minion of the powerful as propagandists are. He was putting forward, as he had every right to, his own view about a shared reality, frankly acknowledging his perspective. Further, he was encouraging viewers to look critically at their government's words and actions. (Potentially weakening this encouragement, however, was his calculated performance of working-class rage, which can lead viewers to see themselves not as social actors but merely as disempowered victims of the powerful.)

Other recent documentaries for public knowledge and action use techniques designed to attract interest across lines of belief. Eugene Jarecki's *Why We Fight* (2005) showcases an argument about the collusion between politicians, big business, and the military to spend the public's money and lives for wars that do not need to be fought. Jarecki deliberately chose Republican subjects, who could transcend partisan politics and speak to the public interest. In Davis Guggenheim's *An Inconvenient Truth* (2006), Al Gore and Davis

Guggenheim, in an easy-to-understand presentation, let scientific data speak to the urgency of the issue. The director of the NASA Goddard Institute for Space Studies, Jim Hansen, noted the public value of the work: "Al Gore may have done for global warming what *Silent Spring* did for pesticides. He will be attacked, but the public will have the information needed to distinguish our long-term well-being from short-term special interests."

Styles can be dramatically different, in order to accomplish the end of public engagement. Judith Helfand and Dan Gold's *Blue Vinyl* (2002) employs the personal diary format to personalize a problem. The film follows Helfand as she takes a piece of her parents' home's vinyl siding and discovers the cancer-causing toxicity of vinyl at the beginning and end of its life cycle (it creates dioxin). Helfand becomes a representative of the public—people who need inexpensive siding and also suffer the health consequences of using it. Brazilian José Padilha's *Bus 174* (2002),

1. *Blue Vinyl* used personal essay to explore social issues; Judith Helfand—a piece of her suburban home's vinyl siding in hand—explores toxic effects of vinyl production. Directed by Daniel B. Gold and Judith Helfand, 2002.

in retelling a sensational news event in Rio de Janeiro—the hijacking of a bus, a several-hour standoff, and ultimate death of both hijacker and a bus rider, telecast live—brings viewers both into the life of the hijacker and the challenges of the police. By contrasting television footage that had glued viewers to their sets for an entire day along with investigations into the stories leading up to the event, the film reframes the "news" as an example of how endemic and terrible social problems are turned into spectacle. *Three Rooms of Melancholia* (2005), an epic meditation by Finnish filmmaker Pirjo Honkasalo, draws viewers into the Russian war against Chechnya by creating an emotional triptych. In "Longing," her camera caresses the earnest faces of twelve-year-old cadets in St. Petersburg, training to fight Chechens; in the second part, "Breathing," a local social worker visits the sad apartments of Grozny under siege, where daily-life problems become insuperable; the third, "Remembering," takes place in an orphanage just over the border, where Chechnyan young people learn bitterness. Little is said; in contemplative close-up, the faces of puzzlement, pain, and endurance speak volumes. The viewer has become complicit with the camera in knowing.

Whether a filmmaker intends to address the public or not, documentaries may be used in unexpected ways. One of the most infamous propaganda films of all time, *Triumph of the Will* (1935), has had a long life in other, anti-Nazi propaganda and in historical films. Israeli Yo'av Shamir's *Checkpoint* (2003), a scrupulously observed, non-narrated record of the behavior of Israeli troops at Palestinian checkpoints, was intended and was used as a provocation to public discussion of human rights violations. The Israeli Army embraced it as a training film.

Our shared understanding of what a documentary is—built up from our own viewing experience—shifts over time, with business and marketing pressures, technological and formal innovations, and with vigorous debate. The genre of documentary always has two crucial elements that are in tension: representation, and reality. Their makers manipulate and distort reality like all filmmakers, but they still make a claim for making a truthful representation of reality. Throughout the history of documentary film, makers, critics, and viewers have argued about what constitutes trustworthy storytelling about reality. This book introduces you to those arguments over time and in some of its popular subgenres.

Form

What does a documentary look like? Most people carry inside their heads a rough notion of what a documentary is. For many of them, it is not a pretty picture. "A "regular documentary" often means a film that features sonorous, "voice-of-God" narration, an analytical argument rather than a story with characters, head shots of experts leavened with a few people-on-the-street interviews, stock images that illustrate the narrator's point (often called "b-roll" in broadcasting), perhaps a little educational animation, and dignified music. This combination of formal elements is not usually remembered fondly. "It was really interesting, not like a regular documentary," is a common response to a pleasant theatrical experience.

In fact, documentarians have a large range of formal choices in registering for viewers the veracity and importance of what they show them. The formal elements many associate with "regular documentary" are part of a package of choices that became standard practice in the later twentieth century on broadcast television, but there are quite a few more to be had. This chapter provides you with several ways to consider the documentary as a set of decisions about how to represent reality with the tools available to the filmmaker. These tools include *sound* (ambient sound, soundtrack music, special sound effects, dialogue, narration); *images* (material shot on location, historical images captured in photographs, video, or objects); *special effects* in audio and video, including animation; and *pacing* (length of scenes, number of cuts, script or storytelling structure). Filmmakers choose the way they want to structure a story—which characters to develop for viewers, whose stories to focus on, how to resolve the storytelling.

Filmmakers have many choices to make about each of the elements. For instance, a single shot may be framed differently and carry a different meaning depending on the frame: a close-up of a father grieving may say something quite different from a wide shot of the same scene showing the entire room; a decision to let the ambient sound of the funeral dominate the soundtrack will mean something different than a swelling soundtrack.

Since there is nothing natural about the representation of reality in documentary, documentary filmmakers are acutely aware that all their choices shape the meaning they choose. All documentary conventions—that is, habits or clichés in the formal choices of expression—arise from the need to convince viewers of the authenticity of what they are being told. For instance, experts vouch for the truthfulness of analysis; dignified male narrators signify authority for many viewers; classical music connotes seriousness.

Challenges to conventions stake an alternative claim to authenticity. At a time when ambient sound could be collected only with difficulty, conventions of 35mm sound production included authoritatively delivered narration. They also included lighting and even staging, appropriate to the heavy, difficult-to-move equipment. Some documentaries used careful editing between the crafted compositions of each scene, to create the illusion of reality before the viewer's eyes. When filmmakers began experimenting with lighter 16mm equipment after World War II, the conventions that arose differently persuaded viewers of the documentary's truthfulness. Using very long "takes" or scenes made viewers feel that they were watching unvarnished reality; the jerkiness of handheld cameras was testimony to the you-are-there immediacy, and it implied urgency; "ambush" interviews, catching subjects on the fly or by surprise, led viewers to believe that the subject must be hiding something. The choice against narration, which became fashionable in the later 1960s, allowed viewers to believe that they were being allowed to decide for themselves the meaning of what they saw (even though editing choices actually controlled what they saw).

Documentarians employ the same techniques as do fiction filmmakers. Cinematographers, sound technicians, digital designers, musicians, and editors may work in both modes. Documentary work may require lights, and directors may ask their subjects for retakes; documentaries usually require sophisticated editing; documentarians add sound effects and sound tracks.

A shared convention of most documentaries is the narrative structure. They are stories, they have beginnings, middles, and ends; they invest viewers in their characters, they take viewers on emotional journeys. They often refer to classic story structure. When Jon Else made a documentary about J. Robert Oppenheimer, the creator of the first atomic bomb—a scientist who anguished over his responsibilities—Else had his staff read *Hamlet*.

Conventions work well to command attention, facilitate storytelling, and share a maker's perspective with audiences. They become the aesthetic norm—off-the-shelf choices for documentarians, shortcuts to register truthfulness. Conventions also, however, disguise the assumptions that makers bring to the project, and make the presentation of the particular facts and scenes seem both inevitable and complete.

Showcasing convention

How, then, to see formal choices as choices, to see conventions as conventions? You may turn to films whose makers put formal choice front and center as subject matter, and contrast their choices with more routine work.

One of the easiest ways to see conventions is through satire and parody. For example, the great Spanish surrealist artist Luis Buñuel's *Land without Bread (Las Hurdes: Tierra sin Pan*, 1932) begins as a seemingly tedious, pompous excursion into an impoverished corner of Spain. Soon, however, it becomes clear that Buñuel, aided by the commentary written by the surrealist artist Pierre Unik, is using dry, pseudo-scientific conventions to incite bewilderment and outrage, both at the narrator and then at the horrific social conditions of the countryside. The British Broadcasting Company (BBC)'s 1957 *The Spaghetti Story*, a segment in its *Panorama* series, takes viewers to Switzerland to discuss the latest spaghetti harvest (growing on trees) as a joke that also functions as a media literacy lesson. The wry *In Search of the Edge* (1990), purportedly about why the earth is flat, employs a wide range of educational-documentary devices that people associate with "regular documentary"—all with deliberate clumsiness—to demonstrate false logic in scientific arguments and manipulation in filmmaking. Here, experts are given such titles as "university professor" and are shown in front of bookcases signifying scholarship, although they speak nonsense; flashy graphics demonstrate physical impossibilities; the narrator's tone is contemptuous of the notion that the earth is round; a family photo is shown in gradual close-up, Ken Burns–style, only to show the mentioned character with her head turned. The Australian film *Babakiueria* (1988), made by an aboriginal group, satirizes ethnographic film conventions, including the ascribing of mysterious or magical properties to exotic others in narration, the expert witness, the pretentious narrator, and the portrayal of scientific investigation as heroic exploration. In the film, aboriginal scientists investigate what they believe to be a white Australian cultural ritual site, which actually is a barbecue area.

Mockumentaries, or tongue-in-cheek fake documentaries, also offer the chance to see conventions at an angle. Rob Reiner's *This Is Spinal Tap!* (1984), about an imaginary heavy metal band, famously parodied rockumentaries—performance films of rock bands—with their contrast of high-energy stage performance with goofy backstage antics and their populist success narratives. Like later mockumentaries such as *Best in Show* (2000) and *A Mighty Wind* (2003), the humor depended on the audience being able to identify the conventions.

Artistic experiment

Another way to see conventions is to analyze films by makers who see themselves primarily as artists—makers manipulating form rather than storytellers using the film medium—as they invent, reinvent, and challenge. Where the market pressures of attracting audiences have led many filmmakers to employ familiar conventions, artists working outside the film and video marketplaces have sought to go beyond them. They are frontline innovators and experimenters.

One highly celebrated example of such artistic countercurrents is the city symphony film. In the 1920s and 1930s, when theaters were showing nature adventures, war newsreels, and exotica, artists producing for galleries in interwar Europe imagined cinema (then a silent medium) as, among other things, a visual poem, one that could unite the experience of different senses. It was a time of exuberant experimentation and international communication. City symphonies participated in the modernist love of the urban, of machinery, and of progress. They absorbed elements from artistic movements such as surrealism and futurism, and they let people see what they usually could not or would not. Among the machines artists loved was the camera itself, which represented a superior "mechanical eye," as Russian documentarian and theorist Dziga Vertov called it. An early example of the city symphony was Paul Strand and Charles Sheeler's *Manhatta* (1921), and the form proliferated on the European continent in the later 1920s.

The city symphony was given its name by the German filmmaker Walther Ruttmann's *Berlin: Symphony of a Great City* (1927). Ruttmann also commissioned a score for the film. The very term "city symphony" unites the brash industrial enterprise of the modern city with the classical musical form that demonstrates the capacity to organize and coordinate many individual expressions into a whole. The film takes the viewer into Berlin on a train and then on a day-long tour of the many urban patterns emerging from the interaction of people and machines, culminating with fireworks. In the film, Ruttmann experimented with Vertov's ideas about the power of documentary to be an "eye" on society in a way that transcended the power of human observation.

Many artists seized upon the city symphony notion as a way of experimenting with the medium. The Brazilian artist Alberto Cavalcanti was inspired by the project Ruttmann was developing and made *Rien que les Heures* (1926), a film about Paris, even before Ruttmann completed his. It features clever special effects in a whirlwind tour of Paris that includes both the highest and lowest classes of society. In the south of France, Vertov's exiled younger brother, Boris Kaufman, and the French artist Jean Vigo, produced a slyly satirical little film, *À Propos de Nice* (1930), showing the beach town as a self-indulgent culture of gambling and sun- and self-worshiping. (Vertov wrote filmmaking instructions to his brother.) In Belgium, Henri Storck made a closely observed film about his own beach town, in *Images d'Ostende* (1930), and the Dutch filmmaker Joris Ivens, who went on to work with Storck, made what became a classic of these films, *Rain*. Vertov, in touch with these developments, created his masterpiece, *Man with a Movie Camera*.

The city symphony form remains an unusual, poetic choice, an exception to the rule of documentary conventions. Godfrey Reggio's 1982 *Koyaanisqatsi* uses lightshow-like techniques along with time-lapse photography (one of the techniques pioneered by city symphony films) to make a histrionic commentary on mankind's devastating effect on the earth. The title refers to a Hopi word meaning "life out of balance." American film scholar Thom Andersen used nearly a century of cinema to look at how Los

Angeles has been represented in the movies in *Los Angeles Plays Itself* (2003). It sometimes wryly, sometimes bleakly shows the city in the commercial and public imagination.

Other self-described artists have searched for ways to use documentary film as a road to purity of vision and a celebration of the ecstasy of sensation itself. Because their films deliberately eschew conventions such as story line, narrator, and sometimes even discernable objects in the world, they provide another way of understanding what we have come to expect. Kenneth Anger, Jonas Mekas, Carolee Schneeman, Jordan Belson, and Michael Snow all made films that creatively interpreted real life, although they identified themselves as avant-garde artists and not documentarians. One of the best known American avant-garde artists who did think of himself as a documentarian—and a scientist—was Stan Brakhage.

Brakhage wanted viewers to return to an "innocent eye," a purity of experience of vision. He wanted to help people *see*, not only what the eye takes in from the outside but also what the eye creates as a result of memory or bodily energy from the inside. "I really think my films are documentaries. All of them," he said. "They are my attempts to get as accurate a representation of seeing as I possibly can." Most of Brakhage's work was silent and executed in the passionate belief that seeing was a full-body action. Surprisingly, his artistic intuitions and perceptions of how the eye works are supported by scientific research on optics.

Brakhage made hundreds of films; two of the most seen are *Mothlight* (1963) and *The Garden of Earthly Delights* (1981). In both short films, Brakhage encased found natural objects, put them between two pieces of celluloid and then printed the images created. *Mothlight* contained moth wings; *Garden* contained twigs, flowers, seeds, and weeds. The images produced then created an experience for viewers, which referred to the original but was entirely different.

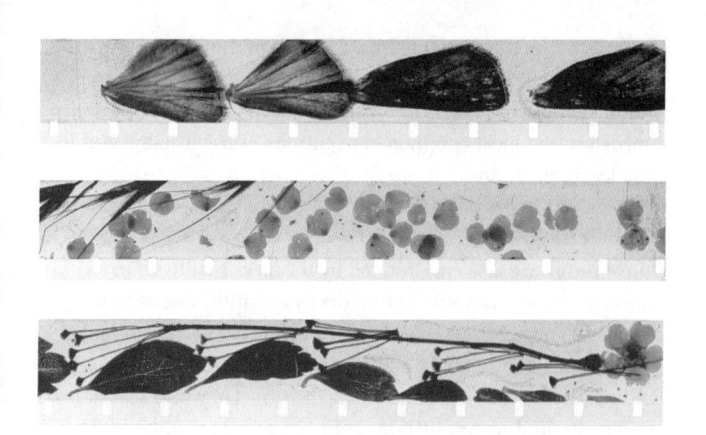

2. In *Mothlight*, experimental documentarian Stan Brakhage pressed moth wings and scraps of twigs and flowers between celluloid strips. Directed by Stan Brakhage, 1963.

Art films have also experimented with sound. The German experimental filmmaker Hans Richter translated sound rhythms into visual experience in the 1920s and 1930s. The Indian filmmaker Mani Kaul, who grew up artistically in India's subsidized "parallel cinema" (i.e., parallel to commercial cinema) in the 1970s, has worked repeatedly with Indian song traditions, including *Dhrupad* (1982), which mesmerizes with the sound and image of one classical music performance style designed to facilitate spiritual meditation. Such work highlights the way in which we often take sound for granted as a convenient emotional conductor.

In all these works, the conventions of "regular documentary" are largely absent. No narrator tells us what is going on; no experts provide authority; ordinary reality is deliberately distorted so that we will see it differently; soundtracks are used for other purposes than cueing story-linked emotions. Patterns of light and dark, the hypnotic sound of repetitive music, the sight of objects from the natural world projected at many times their size, and other devices shock us out of our visual habits. These experiments have greatly expanded the repertoire of formal approaches for documentary filmmakers. At the same time, these experiments provide a sharp contrast to the most common conventions, those usually used in broadcast television.

Economic context

Conventions are also conditioned by business realities. On television, where viewers make a decision within one or two seconds about whether to watch, producers now strive to make every moment compelling and to signal brand identity not only through identifying logos but through style. They also search for ways to streamline production and reduce costs through style and form. A History Channel executive in the later 1990s memorably explained that channel's then-formula—clips either of stock footage or of small staged scenes or objects interpolated with talking heads and stitched together with narration—to a group of striving producers: "We do it because it's cheap and it works."

Filmmakers have looked to three kinds of funders to pay for their documentaries: *patrons* or *sponsors*, both corporate and governmental; *advertisers*, typically on television and usually at one remove; and *users* or *audiences*. Each source of funding has powerfully affected the choices of filmmakers.

Government sponsors have been critically important to documentary filmmaking. In the British Commonwealth, institutions that promote the making and distribution of documentary film include the BBC, the Australian Broadcasting Corporation, and the Canadian National Film Board. Throughout continental Europe, governments provide subsidies to artists who work on documentaries. German, French, and Dutch documentary work has flourished with this kind of investment. In the developing world, ex-colonial powers sometimes provide stipends for cultural production; national governments may offer resources and often control access to screens. Cultural nationalism is a powerful motive for national governments to provide these subsidies. Programming themes and styles often reflect a concern to express national identity, especially against the unceasing international flow of U.S. popular media.

By contrast, U.S. taxpayer support for documentary has historically been anemic, in a nation where cultural policy has always strongly supported commercial media. U.S. public broadcasting was given a rebirth in the liberal heyday of Lyndon Johnson's Great Society, with committed public funds for the noncommercial, nongovernmental entity to help build capacity of the then-feeble public broadcast stations in most major cities. During the 1970s and 1980s, other cultural organizations, especially the taxpayer-funded National Endowment for the Humanities and the National Endowment for the Arts, also contributed to American documentary. Unconventional styles, themes, and politically sensitive topics often raised conservative ire in Congress.

Another way in which governments have been important to documentary filmmaking is through regulation that encourages certain kinds of production over others. For example, when the British government authorized the existence of private commercial television channels, it also required hefty public interest responsibilities, which translated into ambitious documentary projects funded in hopes of prestige, recognition, and license renewal. British Channel 4 was launched with funds siphoned from advertising revenues of a commercial channel and was given a mandate to feature the work of independent producers, including many documentarians. Chad Raphael has argued that American broadcast network fear of government regulation (networks had been caught rigging quiz shows) led to a period of lavish funding for investigative public affairs documentaries. (Indeed, the decline of government regulation of television in the 1980s resulted in a decline in public affairs documentaries.)

Government regulators play a de facto role in standards-setting and enforcing of conventions. Broadcasters are usually under tight scrutiny by regulators who patrol use of airwaves, which the government typically leases to individual companies with conditions. In a documentary about drug smuggling, *The Connection,* Brian Winston recounted a scandal that erupted in Britain in 1998 over re-created or possibly even fictional footage. The British Independent Television Commission, a regulatory body, fined the television channel that aired the film and set in motion debates about government censorship.

The U.S. Federal Communications Commission (FCC) levied an indecency fine, widely criticized as arbitrary, on a public television station for airing a history program, *The Blues* (2003), because in it a jazz musician uttered a vulgar word. The judgment then made many broadcasters even more cautious in their programming.

The role of private-sector sponsors in the history of documentary has been large, and surely will continue to be. Key works of documentary founder Robert Flaherty were backed by corporate sponsors who hoped to associate their image with his romantic vision. Corporate underwriters and sponsors were also essential to early documentary on television. For instance, the American public affairs program featuring the great journalist Edward R. Murrow, *See It Now* (1951), was funded by Alcoa, which at the time was looking to burnish its reputation after an antitrust suit. Corporate underwriters have been crucial to public service television as well. Nonprofit organizations have also become significant clients for documentary film work on issues they consider important. Sponsors pay to have a film made because they want a particular story told or they want to improve their image. Either way, a filmmaker has limited autonomy but often it is enough to be able to do important work. Sometimes a filmmaker's priorities accord well with an organization's, as well. Advertisers are also sponsors, each of whom pays for a little time or space on a program that can attract viewers to their messages. Advertising favors lightweight, low-budget documentaries that do not challenge the status quo and sensationalist documentaries that can drive up ratings.

Direct sale is the fastest-growing model for documentary support. Theatrical audiences looking for novelty and awe find it in IMAX documentaries, whether on the miracle of flight or the astounding world of tropical insects. Subscribers to cable channels, such as HBO or Canada's Doc Channel, receive a flow of documentary programming the same way they subscribe to magazines. Video on demand also offers documentaries direct to viewers, as do rental services such as Netflix and Blockbuster. Home users are purchasing, often online, DVDs of documentaries that may never have seen the inside of a theater, and they are also downloading films to their video iPods and cell phones; this drives documentarians to identify a "personal audience," as producer Peter Broderick calls it, and to craft work around the interests of this niche or identify a constituency passionate about a particular cause or issue.

A breakthrough example of direct distribution was the Robert Greenwald–produced *Outfoxed* (2004), which lambastes Fox News for its right-wing bias. Launched during the 2004 election season in the United States, this film was offered to viewers via e-mails from the liberal website MoveOn.org. According to organizers, more than 100,000 viewers purchased the DVDs within the month, mostly for use in house parties where several viewers saw it at once. The film also received a limited, simultaneous theatrical run. The example was rapidly imitated and tweaked; soon conservatives were making their own incendiary films and circulating them to their constituencies.

Digital production in a download era bids fair to develop new market models. By 2006 video downloads occupied perhaps half the total traffic on the Internet. Within days, obscure homemade parodies have drawn worldwide audiences larger than many documentaries ever gained in a festival and theatrical run. At the same time, the business model that can support such work still remained to be seen.

Ethics and form

Ethical issues have been as critical as aesthetic ones in the formal choices of documentarians. American historical filmmaker Jon Else and theorist Bill Nichols among others have called for professional filmmakers themselves to articulate ethical standards.

One ongoing question is that of how much simulation of reality is acceptable. Outright fakery is easy to condemn, although it is common from the origins of film: Thomas Edison's studio produced war footage from the Philippines in New Jersey, and the supposed record of the sinking of the *Maine* in the Havana harbor was actually filmed in a New York bathtub.

Other practices are less ethically clear. Reenactment was a staple of 35mm documentary film production. Given the cumbersome machinery, without lighting and staging, most filmmaking of this kind would have been impossible. Cinema verité purists in the 1960s, using new lighter-weight and more-flexible equipment, scorned such techniques, denigrating them as artificial.

Reenactment burgeoned again, though, in the 1990s. Sometimes, it was because of the low budgets offered by cable programmers that filmmakers struggled to produce compelling storytelling for television audiences used to high production values. Thus, on the History Channel, for example, it became common for a few feet in sandals to represent the march of thousands of Roman warriors, or for a few coins and a vase to represent the wealth of kings in another era. Other times, filmmakers used reenactment to evoke an uncaptured moment. In the Holocaust-memoir film *Tak for Alt* (1999), scenes of a mother making challah and lighting candles were staged to represent the memories of the survivor's childhood. Such use is not confusing to viewers, since they usually can distinguish what is genuine experience from the symbolic representation of it.

Controversy has grown up around filmmaking in which the fake is interwoven with the real, without giving viewers the chance to distinguish. The civil rights history *Mighty Times: Volume 2: The Children's March* (2004), by Robert Hudson and Bobby Houston, intermixed reenactments and archival material, and also used archival material from one place and time to signify another. When it won an Academy Award, the film generated controversy for its intermixing. David McNab's *The Secret Plot to Kill Hitler* (2004) was part of a Discovery Channel experiment in "virtual history," in which actors reenact a moment in history, and the heads of historical figures are borrowed from archival footage. The film admitted this at the outset, but some believed the approach of mixing actors with archival images crossed an ethical line and could potentially confuse people.

Films that throughout use actors and scripts, with creative license, to retell true events are usually called docudramas. Films such as *Gandhi* (1982) or television series such as *Roots* (1977) are docudramas. They look and feel like fiction films, and it is generally understood that they can take some license with details in order to dramatically represent a reality. However, neither viewers nor journalists think falsifying reality is appropriate. A 2006 ABC network docudrama, *The Path to 9/11*, cast actors in roles of real Clinton administration officials, including that of the secretary of state, and had them say and do things that they clearly had not. These falsifications showed the Clinton administration neglecting a terrorist threat. The network deleted some errors at the last minute and then tried to absolve itself by noting that the film was only a docudrama, but outraged viewers and commentators were not mollified by the disclaimer.

Some documentaries mix in fictional elements while still laying claim to being documentaries. This style is growing with the popularity of documentary entertainment. For example, Danish filmmaker Jeppe Rønde's *The Swenkas* (2004) tells a fable about a father-and-son reunion, within documentation of real-life male fashion contests in South Africa. Although it was popular in film festivals in the global North, the film raises questions for its representation of a fictional plot as real life.

Some documentary filmmakers deliberately use fiction as a provocation. British left-wing filmmaker Peter Watkins has made many films using nonactors to reenact historical incidents that reveal structures of power and movements of resistance, from the Battle of Culloden to the Paris Commune. American radical filmmaker Emile de Antonio in his *In the King of Prussia* (1982) restaged a trial of anti-Vietnam War protesters, after reporters were banned from the courtroom. The film starred the actual defendants, including the priestly brothers Philip and Daniel Berrigan, with the Hollywood actor Martin Sheen as the judge. The reenactment not only retold the events but implicitly critiqued the banning of reporters during the trial. The French filmmaker Chris Marker, in his *Sans Soleil* (1982) mixed documentary images and sound with a fictional narration. The result was a provocative inquiry into the meaning of memory and a meditation on filmmaking. In *Perfumed Nightmare* (1977), Philippine filmmaker Kidlat Tahimik recycled documentary footage to tell a fictional story about a Third World innocent who traveled to the West—a tale that was also a critical documentary essay about the interpenetration of West and East. The recycling itself was a commentary on the Philippines' syncretic and eclectic culture.

German artist Harun Farocki has created many complex and self-reflexive film essays where documentary footage is used and wrenching questions of public importance addressed. His essay on the complicity of industrial workers in the Vietnam war, *Nicht löschbares Feuer* (*The Indistinguishable Fire*, 1969)—the fire referred to napalm—was scripted and staged in a style that attempted Brechtian alienation. American filmmaker Jill

Godmilow later remade the film shot-for-shot as *What Farocki Taught* (1998).

Are such hybrids still documentary? Like the mainstream of documentary, they claim to portray real life, telling the viewer something important about it. But to some, these experiments are outside the bounds of documentary, as are mockumentaries. Godmilow herself, within her film, asks the viewer what kind of movie *What Farocki Taught* is. She points out that almost all scenes were reenacted, such as most scenes in the film it mimics had been, and yet the film is an argument about real life. She suggests, partly tongue in cheek, that the viewer regard the film as "agit-prop," recalling the Soviet-era term for "agitation-propaganda" films to incite social change. Her own questioning points to the fuzzy lines around the border of the genre.

Filmmakers' formal choices all make persuasive claims to the viewer about the accuracy, good faith, and reasonableness of the filmmaker. The fact that filmmakers have a wide variety of choices in representing reality is a reminder that there is no transparent representation of reality. No one can solve these ethical dilemmas by eschewing choice in expression, and no formal choices are wrong in themselves. A good-faith relationship between maker and viewer is essential. Filmmakers can facilitate that by being clear to themselves why they are using the techniques that they do, and striving for formal choices that honor the reality they want to share.

Founders

Three figures who launched their careers in the 1920s have shaped expectation of audiences worldwide ever since: Robert Flaherty, John Grierson, and Dziga Vertov. Each one claimed simultaneously that they told the truth and that they were artists. These two assertions, as we have seen, create the most basic tension in documentary. When does artistry conflict with reality and when does it facilitate such representation? These filmmakers variously grappled with that question and set the stage for later arguments.

Grierson and Flaherty, with different aspirations, both anchored a tradition of *realism* in documentary. This expressive tradition creates the illusion of reality for the viewer. Thus, realism was not an attempt to authentically capture reality but an attempt to use art to mimic it so effectively that the viewer would be pulled in without thinking about it. Some of the techniques to create the illusion of reality include (1) elision editing (editing that goes unnoticed by the conscious mind, so that your eye is tricked into thinking it is merely moving with the action); (2) cinematography that creates the illusion that you are almost in the scene or "looking over the shoulder" of the action and gives you a psychological stake in the action; and (3) pacing that follows the viewer's expectations for events in the natural world. Because of its evocative power, realism has become the international language of commercial cinema, in both documentary and fiction.

In contrast to realism are approaches that call attention to the artist's and the technology's role in creating the film. Some of these approaches have been grouped under the term *formalism*, meaning the highlighting of formal elements in the film itself. Examples of such elements include sharp or recognizable edits, unnatural colors, distortions in the lens, special effects such as animation, and slowing down or speeding up sound and image. In the early days of film, many filmmakers experimented with these techniques, and they have typified a strong strand of expression in documentary outside commercial strictures ever since. (Advertisers have also found them helpful, for memorable, high-impact effects.) Proponents of formalism charged realists with illusionism, with tricking viewers into believing that they are watching something real; instead, these makers argued, let viewers notice and even celebrate the artist's role in creating the work.

Robert Flaherty

The American Robert Flaherty produced only a few films in a lifetime's work, but some have become touchstones of documentary. His first film, *Nanook of the North,* was a popular success and inspired filmmakers all over the world, from the Russian Sergei Eisenstein to the British John Grierson to the French Jean Rouch.

Flaherty grew up in and on the border of Canada, living partly in mining camps with his father, a mine owner. After an aborted film (the negative burned up) made as documentation of his travels, he returned for a year to the indigenous Arctic people who had treated him well, with funds from a French fur trading company. Although several distributors turned down the resulting film, the film made a great deal of money both for itself and for Flaherty. *Nanook* was promoted in theaters with gimmicks such as dogsleds and cardboard displays of igloos, and it was touted as "a story of life and love in the actual Arctic."

The film borrowed from popular screen entertainment of the time. It had "scenic" elements of the popular travelogue film, itself a legatee of travel slide shows. It told a dramatic story of survival against the elements, using a similar structure to that of the fiction feature by D. W. Griffith, *Birth of a Nation* (1915), which Flaherty had seen. It also had novelty: Flaherty introduced viewers to daily life in a culture that both he and his audiences thought of as primitive. The novelty of the film was that the "primitives" were not shown as freaks or exotic animals (as they had been only recently at the Chicago World Columbian Exhibition in 1893) but as people with families and communities. Urban audiences could look over the filmmaker's shoulder to see into another way of life—indeed, they believed, even into the past. Flaherty's representation of Inuit lifestyle was deliberately archaic.

Nanook's warm humanism was a far more commercially successful approach than that of another "salvage ethnographer," the photographer Edward S. Curtis, whom the Flahertys had visited before finishing *Nanook*. Curtis, already renowned for his photography of American Indians in archaic dress, had hoped to pay for years of living with Kwakiutl Indians with a film that would attract paying audiences. His *In the Land of the Headhunters* (1914)—later renamed, more accurately, *In the Land of the War Canoes*—combined footage of rites that he had asked the Kwakiutl to revive with a melodramatic plot that did not draw from Kwakiutl culture. It was a sad and clumsy box office and aesthetic failure, although of immense interest to later anthropologists for its re-created ritual scenes.

Flaherty clearly made some choices with the goal of engaging ticket-paying audiences. He renamed Allakariallak as Nanook and assembled for him a photogenic but fake nuclear family. He disguised the participation of various Inuit in the making of the film. He featured and even staged high-drama hunts rather than record the more-uneventful pace of daily life, particularly that of the women. Flaherty's camerawork—the product of meticulous visual care and many retakes—and the editor's clever pacing (slow enough to convince viewers they were watching real life, but dramatically shaped) produced high-quality entertainment from compelling raw material. The choice of a realist mode—creating, as it were, the illusion of seen and felt reality through editing, camera angle, and pacing—gave viewers a vivid impression of having virtually experienced something genuine.

Flaherty's archaism in the film was a moral choice. "What I want to show," he said, "is the former majesty and character of these people, while it is still possible—before the white man has destroyed not only their character, but the people as well." Flaherty had a powerful romantic belief in the purity of native cultures, and he believed that his own culture was spiritually impoverished by comparison. "Nanook's problem was how to live with nature,"

Flaherty's widow recalled him saying. "Our problem is how to live with our machines. Nanook found the solution of the problem in his own spirit, as the Polynesians did in theirs. But we have made for ourselves an environment that is difficult for the spirit to come to terms with."

This romantic conviction also meant that Flaherty believed Inuit culture was polluted by contact with the outside world; he did not believe that Inuit culture could survive the onslaught. For him, true native culture was pure, untouched by machine-made civilization, even though the very Inuit he depended on to fix his cameras were also selling to fur markets.

And that romanticism became a mark of Flaherty's work. He made, among others, *Moana* (1926) in Samoa, *Man of Aran* (1934) on the

3. Romantic realist Robert Flaherty asked Inuit to re-create traditional customs for *Nanook of the North*. Directed by Robert Flaherty, 1922.

desolate Aran Islands off Ireland, and *Louisiana Story* (1948), his last film, in the bayous of Louisiana. Each of these films erased the complexities of social relationships in favor of a narrative of man against nature. In the South Seas, Flaherty was flummoxed to discover that nature was forgiving to the islanders, so he created drama in the then-dying custom of painful tattooing. He ignored, among other things, the colonial presence in Samoa, the aggressive privatization of property that transformed Samoan communities, and the governmental insistence on Western legal marriage that contravened Samoans' own marital traditions. In *Man of Aran* (1934), Flaherty got Aran Islanders to revive the hunting of basking sharks (they had to be taught), and excluded from the story two elements that largely conditioned their lives: their fish trade with the mainland, and the fact that it was absentee landlords and not the harsh forces of nature that forced his subjects onto the poor land that they needed to enrich with seaweed.

One reason for *Nanook*'s appeal is Flaherty's celebration of the "noble savage," a popular notion with a long heritage in Western thought, going back to the early Enlightenment and expressed in Jean-Jacques Rousseau's writing. The noble savage notion expresses an optimism that natural man is inherently good. It had become particularly vivid in the European and Anglo-American imagination at the height of European colonialism in the Victorian era and with the American "manifest destiny" ideology. Even as rising powers asserted political domination over different cultures, their explorers pursued untouched exotic lands beyond their knowledge and celebrated the beauty of the simple life. As Leo Marx has noted, this romantic view of other cultures valued for their supposed simplicity and innocence only grew with rapid industrialization.

Another reason why people continue to love Flaherty's films is that Flaherty's immense affection for his subjects is palpable. Flaherty established a warm human bond with the people he lived and worked with for months at a time. Four decades after Flaherty made *Man of Aran*, filmmaker George Stoney—who had been inspired to take up filmmaking by watching Flaherty's films—returned to the island where his grandfather had been the first physician to interview people who had worked on the film. His *How the Myth Was Made* (1978) examines *Man of Aran* as a myth artfully crafted out of reality. Still, people there recalled Flaherty with great affection. Generations of Inuit have also watched *Nanook* with pleasure, regarding it as a gift allowing them to know their traditions.

Reviewers at the time raised questions about intention and ethics, particularly concerning *Man of Aran*. Grierson and Paul Rotha, another leader of what came to be called the British documentary, celebrated Flaherty as a great artist who elevated documentary to be beautiful art rather than a mere record. For these two filmmakers, Flaherty lacked the social conscience and commitment to adaptation to the industrial age that typified their movement. In the middle of the Great Depression, Flaherty's work irritated left-of-center critics. "Man's struggle with Nature is incomplete unless it embraces the struggle of man with man," leftist British critic Ivor Montagu wrote. "No less than Hollywood, Flaherty is busy turning reality into romance. The tragedy is that, being a poet with a poet's eye, his lie is the greater, for he can make the romance seem real."

After Flaherty's death, critical opinion developed into two camps, which anthropologist Jay Ruby has called "Flaherty the myth" and "Flaherty the romantic fraud." Flaherty's widow, Frances, an indispensable enabler of all his projects, became the guardian of the flame. She celebrated what she called "The Flaherty Way," which she described as a special ability to "surrender to the material," so that Flaherty could share with viewers his "innocent eye" on the subject matter. She coined the term "non-preconception" to describe his approach—which she typified as intuitive, mystical, unerring. Helen van Dongen, Flaherty's editor for his last two projects and the person who had carved stories out of footage, rejected the mystical claims of Frances Flaherty but celebrated him as a "visionary poet," a "genius," and an artist whose career was sadly crippled by the needs of commerce.

The growth of anticolonial consciousness, the rise of a nationalist cultural elite in the Cold War–era Third World, and the growth of self-reflexive anthropology all fueled the "Flaherty the romantic fraud" argument. Some argue that his man-versus-nature theme deepened unhelpful assumptions about indigenous peoples; indigenous people only seem to command our sentimental concern when we can keep them at a safe distance, where they provide a mental vacation for us. The man-versus-nature conflict further fostered an understanding of indigenous people as childlike or even petlike innocents, potential victims before civilization. It led people to look skeptically on political efforts of indigenous people to lay claim to the benefits of their existing relationship with larger economies. Jay Ruby has cautioned anthropologists, however, not to judge Flaherty too harshly before looking at their own practices.

The legacy of Robert Flaherty endures. *The Story of the Weeping Camel* (2003) features a family in the Gobi Desert that saves the life of a camel calf whose mother rejects it by staging a public ritual in which a musician sings to the camel. The story was scripted and invented by the filmmakers, one of whom was Mongolian. They represented life in the Gobi Desert as they imagine it might have been generations ago, with the help of cheerful nonactors in a constructed nuclear family. The film's co-director Luigi Faloni, when asked his inspiration, said confessionally, "Well, you'll laugh at me, but it was *Nanook of the North*."

John Grierson

The career of John Grierson created conflicts and contradictions in documentary practice at least as great as those of Flaherty. Born in Scotland the son of a conservative Calvinist teacher, Grierson took up filmmaking as a powerful tool to address the problem that occupied his life: how to manage social conflicts in a democratic industrial society. After serving in World War I, he saw brutal labor conflicts, taught in a slum school, preached about good works, and finally won a Rockefeller fellowship in the United States. There he was influenced by pundit Walter Lippman, who argued that our increasingly complex society required professionals who could translate issues for the masses, who otherwise would become overwhelmed by the level of expertise needed to address any particular issue. Grierson was also drawn to the budding business of public relations, which had been born with late nineteenth century labor strife. Finally, he saw in Flaherty's *Nanook* a compelling example of the power of film to bring audiences into another reality, and he was captivated by the ever-charming Flaherty himself. Writing about *Moana*, he celebrated its "documentary" quality, definitively naming the genre.

After he returned to Britain, he was able to persuade British officials of the power of documentary. It was a propitious time for such arguments. In 1927 John Reith, another Scot, became the head of the first public service broadcast in the world—the British Broadcasting Corporation, whose mission was educating and improving the public. The Great Depression exacerbated class tensions in Britain and made the alternative of socialism and even Communism seem plausible to many. In the same period, enormous movements of social reform also blossomed, such as those spurred by the New Deal in the United States. Artists of all kinds, especially those such as photographers and filmmakers whose subject matter was reality, saw art as inextricably intertwined with political and social reform.

Grierson was hired by the Empire Marketing Board to promote the very notion of empire. His superior unambiguously stated the point: "For the State, the function of official documentary is to win the consent of this new public for the existing order." After making the only film he would ever direct—*Drifters* (1928), a documentary on herring fishing cannily produced to respond to an official's interest in that business—he hired a group of young men and very few women, including his sister Ruby, to make films both for government and for large corporations. *Industrial Britain* (1932) was an attempt to wean Britons from their nostalgia for a simpler past. Grierson, however, made the mistake of hiring Flaherty to shoot the film. Before getting fired, Flaherty not only overran the budget but shot footage primarily of artisanship that would indeed evoke nostalgia. *Housing Problems* (1935), directed by Edgar Anstey and Ruby Grierson and paid for by a gas company and a housing agency, let slum dwellers explain the misery of their lot and lent support to the project of slum clearance. *Night Mail* (1936), by Basil Wright and Harry Watt with contributions from poet W. H. Auden and composer Benjamin Britten, followed a letter from mailbox to delivery, mostly on a mail train (the interior of the train was a set). It awed viewers with the intricate bureaucratic and industrial complexity of the government service,

4. John Grierson saw documentary as a tool to promote social cohesion and insight; *Night Mail* celebrated the union of man and machine in British postal delivery. Directed by Harry Watt and Basil Wright, 1936.

burnishing the reputation of the post office and underscoring the interlinked nature of modern society.

Grierson and his "boys" vigorously promoted the notion of documentary as a tool of education and social integration, in lectures and writings. In 1932 Grierson celebrated the power of documentary to observe "life itself," using real people who could help others interpret the world and real stories. This he contrasted to the "shim-sham mechanics" and "Woolworth intentions" of Hollywood-acted films. He heralded Flaherty's ability to let reality dictate the story, although he hoped, referring to Flaherty's romanticism, that "the neo-Rousseauianism implicit in Flaherty's work dies with his own exceptional self." The real challenge, he said, was to apply creativity to the "business of ordering most present chaos" and make a statement "which is honest and lucid and deeply felt and which fulfils the best ends of citizenship." To do this, it was important to get beyond a focus on individuals and move along to processes.

Grierson became more strident about the social function of documentary, even at the expense of the "beautiful." In 1942 he asserted, "The documentary idea was not basically a film idea at all" but "a new idea for public education." He saw the state as a fair and neutral body to manage social democracy; he believed that corporations could use public relations for public good, if they depended on the truth. The fact that he endorsed using some of the same techniques as Nazi propagandists did not bother him: "You can be 'totalitarian' for evil and you can also be 'totalitarian' for good." Grierson advocated the firm separation of documentary from entertainment cinema. Believing that Hollywood was unbeatable and unjoinable, he argued that documentary should strive for noncommercial circuits and wholly different expectations among viewers.

Grierson became a consultant both to corporations and to governments, all looking for the latest tools in public relations. His influence was wide. In Canada, where he spent the bulk of World War II, he launched the National Film Board (NFB), which continues today. He consulted with both the U.S. and the British government. His colleague helped establish the Australian National Film Board. He advised leaders of the South African government; unfortunately, as Keyan Tomaselli has documented, there he fell victim to a ploy by pro-apartheid Afrikaners and recommended their proposals in the name of national unity. Grierson's own role as a leader in documentary film, and indeed the British social documentary movement itself, collapsed after World War II. However, his vision of documentary as a social-education project profoundly influenced later makers.

Contemporary criticism of Grierson's work largely focused on questions of effectiveness. Were the films too radical? They featured working people, which was a shock to many in Britain's class-bound society. Were they going to be popular enough? Were they aesthetically daring enough? In response, Paul Rotha claimed in *Documentary Film* that the movement was "this country's most important contribution to the cinema as a whole," and that declaration became accepted wisdom internationally. Grierson became a revered, almost mythic figure of British and Canadian communications history, in part through the promotional efforts of the Griersonians themselves.

Later scholarship enthusiastically took on the challenge of demolishing the myth, as both Ian Aitken and Jack Ellis have well summarized. It also located Grierson in his time and place as an early champion of public relations. Some charged that Rotha's claim ignored competing film efforts of the time and was somewhat self-serving. Others faulted Grierson's work for naiveté about the implications of realism, and noted the male-oriented, middle-class culture celebrated in the films.

Although Grierson sometimes took the posture of and was accused of being a left-winger, later critics noted his conservatism and his desire to maintain the status quo. Joyce Nelson, looking closely at Grierson's performance in Canada, argued that Grierson downplayed Canadian nationalism in service to Commonwealth unity, and that he supported Hollywood's grip on Canadian screens with his separatist strategy for documentaries.

Perhaps Grierson's harshest critic has been British scholar and ex-broadcast journalist Brian Winston, who argued that Grierson's project poisoned the well for the form, which avoided responsibility for its role as truth teller by taking refuge in claims to art—that "creative treatment" of actuality. It did not engage with the challenges of art, however, dodging that responsibility by claiming that it was serving a higher social purpose. It avoided responsibility for that social purpose, its propaganda function, by claiming to be simply a truth teller. Finally, Grierson ignored evidence that his documentaries were not as widely seen as even minor products of commercial cinema, and that the nontheatrical circuit was driven by educational duty rather than appreciation of the documentary form. Griersonian documentaries were in bad faith, reinforcing the interests of those who funded them and stifling creativity. Filmmakers should be free, Winston argued, to tell the stories they think are important, without the pretentious claim of social service or mystical claims to a unique access to truth.

Elizabeth Sussex, who interviewed many of the proponents of Griersonian British documentary, has contended that Grierson's vision of a form that could make viewers aware of their social context was indeed kept alive and handed down to another generation to do differently. Remarkably for a man who had boasted of world-changing, Rotha later said, "I don't think the films themselves are the least bit important. What is important is the sort of spirit which lay behind them."

Later critiques have grown to such prominence because the movement Grierson set in motion and so vigorously promoted left such a large footprint on documentary filmmaking. The writings of this group became key texts for aspiring filmmakers. The institutions Grierson created or inspired, particularly the Canadian National Film Board, have been important to documentary filmmakers. The notion of documentary film as a project with a social purpose at the core, and of the documentarian as an apostle of social progress, has been extremely persuasive, for better or worse. The business model of government or corporate support with noncommercial, nontheatrical distribution became broadly accepted. Flaherty made the rendering of reality an aesthetic virtue, and Grierson made it a social mission.

Dziga Vertov

The third founding figure in documentary is the revolutionary Russian filmmaker Dziga Vertov (Denis Arkadievich Kaufman). Vertov was both a filmmaker and a polemicist on behalf of what in Russia were called "unplayed" (unstaged) films. He championed the unique truth value of "life caught unaware," the unrehearsed moment. He believed that documentary was the perfect medium for revolution, that not only should it flourish but that fiction film be extinguished as a denial of the capacities of the form. As the Russian revolution ossified into dictatorship, he became a liability to the regime, and his work was ignored within the Soviet Union. For a decade after the Russian revolution, however, Vertov was a formative figure of cinema both in Russia and internationally. Although he became a "nonperson" in his home country's cinema history during the Communist era, he remained an enduring inspiration to avant-garde artists and to documentarians everywhere.

Vertov headily mixed claims of art and science for documentary—the essence of the film medium for him. His dream was for film industries to emphasize "the 'unplayed' film over the play-film, to substitute the document for mise-en-scène, to break out of the proscenium of the theatre and to enter the arena of life itself." He saw the camera as "the mechanical I ... the machine showing the world as it is, which only I am able to see." The camera was a cybernetic extension of the weak human capacity for sight; it could see panoramic vistas from great heights, peer into second-story windows, go great distances. He believed, with many others, that Marxism was a new science of society. For him, the magnificent science of the camera was to be merged with revolutionary Marxist analysis in the editing, to make a scientific tool of revolution, what he called a "Communist decoding" of the material. Thus, the power of machine was married to the power of ideology.

Film was the ideal medium for the new communist society being born in Russia, he believed, because it captured the truths of real life, it did not lie to or distract people, and because it exemplified the wondrous machine-driven modernism of which communism was the cutting edge. He disparaged what he called "art" film, meaning fiction entertainment. Vertov was also an avant-garde artist, and that is his lasting identification.

A Jew in an anti-Semitic country, the young Denis Kaufman gave himself the whimsical name Dziga Vertov ("spinning top") while still in college. As a medical student at one of the few places that accepted Jews in the Europe-oriented Petrograd (St. Petersburg), he imbibed the artistic culture of modernism. He encountered Futurism, an avant-garde movement that celebrated the new, the modern, and the machine. And he fell in love with the works of American poet Walt Whitman.

Revolution gave him the opportunity to work on "agit-trains," which sent revolutionary propaganda to fronts of conflict. He worked on newsreels and edited dozens of editions (ten to twenty minutes long) of *Kino-Pravda* (1925), or Cinema Truth. The name echoed that of the party newspaper *Pravda* and also made a claim for documentary's power. The newsreels whisked viewers to far-flung parts of the new Soviet Union, brought them news of political trials, showed them czarist tanks being redeployed to build public works, sports, accidents, and—a favorite—electrification. They celebrated the wonders of the urban, the modern, and the machine.

They were shown throughout the country in front of fiction features, as well as in clubs and screenings in workplaces and rural areas. Vertov saw amazement and awe in the faces of peasants who had never seen a film before.

As he worked on the newsreels, Vertov came to see more and more exciting possibilities in the medium; he became an evangelist for the unplayed or documentary film. He, his editor Elizaveta Svilova, who later became his wife, and his brother Mikhail Kaufman formed a "Council of Three." The Council of Three gathered around them a group of devotees, calling themselves *kinoks*, or cinema-eyes. They issued provocative polemics and pronouncements such as "WE: Variant of a Manifesto," which invited viewers away "from the sweet embraces of romance,/from the poison of the psychological novel,/from the clutches of the theatre of adultery,/with our backsides to music," into "the open, into four dimensions (three plus time)/in search of our own material, our own meter and rhythm."

Although Vertov dogmatically asserted the scientific wonder of the camera-eye and its capacity for truth-telling beyond human dimensions, like Grierson and Flaherty he also argued that the human storyteller was critical: "[I]t is not enough to show bits of truth on the screen, separate frames of truth. These frames must be thematically organized so that the whole is also a truth." Like Flaherty's "innocent eye" of the artist and Grierson's claim to "creative treatment of actuality," Vertov's claim to the editor's right to organize the chaos of real life into a communist truth was permission for the filmmaker to do exactly what he wanted. Each of them made radical claims for the truth-value of their work, all the while portraying the maker of this truthful rendering as an artist who needed the freedom to create.

Vertov wanted to tell a story about the beauty of communist society, and the importance and nobility of the struggle and sacrifice to build it. He was more radical than many others at the time, both in politics and art. Following Trotsky, he demanded a full nationalization and socialization of the economy. His first documentary *Cinema-Eye (Kino-Glaz*, 1924) announced itself to viewers as "The first exploration of/Life caught unawares/ The first non-artificial cinema object/without/scenario/without/ actors or studio." In an intensely edited and hard-to-follow whirligig of images, it decried the continuing evidence of capitalism and corruption in the economy. He made three more films in quick succession, each pushing forward experiments in editing that used juxtaposition to make connections with actuality film.

Vertov's work, so deliberately unconventional and challenging, intrigued and baffled critics, irritated friends, and incited fierce debate among filmmakers. He made many enemies, and he lost his Moscow job. His masterwork, *Man with a Movie Camera*, brought arguments to a head. With his wife and his cinematographer brother Michael, he created one of the most astonishing and provocative pieces of film art of all time. It was intended to be a sweeping panorama of a transformed nation, where unconsciously the daily lives of ordinary people had become part of a magnificent modernist poem. If Walt Whitman had heard America singing, Dziga Vertov heard the Soviet singing.

A city symphony, *Man with a Movie Camera* used a day-in-the-life format, bracketed by a theatrical conceit. The viewer entered with cinemagoers, and the film ended as they departed. In between, the pixieish cinematographer used the camera's magic to take the viewer into intimate settings (a baby being born, a couple getting divorced), across great landscapes, into workplaces and gymnasia. The cinematographer and the editor played visual jokes—special effects produced for the delight of display of the wonders of this new technology, which could reveal by representing.

In the end, the film commented as much on the power and pleasure of the filmmaker as it did on the extraordinary achievements of the new Russian society. It was the practice that went along with Vertov's fiercely argued theory for the transcendent power of documentary film, not only to record society but to see and imagine it differently than deemed possible by mere human beings. Its opening credits boasted its ambition: "This experimental work is directed towards the creation of a genuine, international purely cinematic language, entirely distinct from the language of the theatre and literature."

The work dazzled and delighted artists and critics worldwide, in part because its ambiguities so pleasurably piqued their curiosity and, of course, also reinforced the self-regard of artists. Russian audiences, who increasingly selected among entertaining comedies and dramas from regional film industries as well as international popular films, felt just the opposite; they complained they didn't know what it was about. The film ruined Vertov's already-imperiled future within an increasingly rigid Soviet Union, where both artistic and political experimentation were suppressed. After a formally exhilarating experiment in sound, *Enthusiasm* or *Symphony of the Don Basin* (1931), Vertov found it hard to get work in the government-controlled industry. His rigorous and relentless experimentalism had fallen out of favor, replaced by easy-to-digest platitudes. In his later years he was put to work editing tedious newsreels and documentaries in praise of Stalin.

While Vertov's work generated enormous energy among artistic and political circles in the Soviet Union, it was not widely seen there. *Kino-Glaz* (1924) was only shown once in public. *Forward, Soviet!* (1926) showed briefly in three theaters, without publicity. *One Sixth of the World* (1926) was not shown on first-run screens. *The Eleventh Year* (1928) played to thousands of Ukrainian viewers, and *Man with a Movie Camera* was shown nationally but not appreciated by general audiences. Film pioneer Sergei Eisenstein, who was an early admirer of Vertov, found himself increasingly exasperated by what he called Vertov's "unmotivated camera mischief." (Vertov vigorously

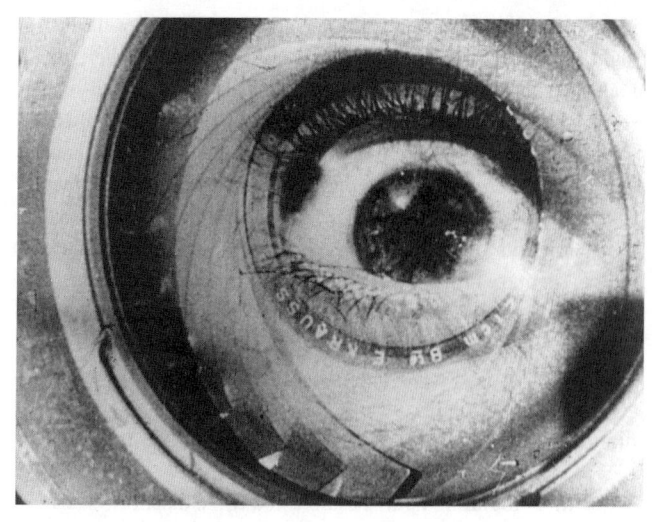

5. Russian revolutionary artist Dziga Vertov experimented with shocking formal techniques in *Man with a Movie Camera*. Directed by Dziga Vertov, 1929.

argued back that Eisenstein needed to respect the power of actuality instead of faking reality in storytelling.)

Vertov's reputation, smothered in the Soviet Union, was kept alive partly by the enthusiasm of Western artists. He was also an important figure to anti-communist writers such as Herbert Marshall, who chronicled his career as one of several "crippled creative biographies" of the USSR. His reputation was also revived by scholars, crucially including film historian Jay Leyda, who witnessed the early years of Russian cinema, and film scholar Annette Michelson, who published and analyzed Vertov's work in English.

Vertov's challenges and his experiments have remained provocative for generations of avant-garde filmmakers: he imagined a film form that transcended the strictures of narrative and naturalist storytelling. The kind of realism that Robert Flaherty chose, implicitly or explicitly telling a struggle-to-survive story, was anathema to Vertov and to filmmakers who wanted to use art to shatter expectations of the status quo. His work and Eisenstein's were important to John Grierson, who was attracted to their claims that film could serve social change. Filmmakers in the 1960s who broke free of what had become staged conventions in documentary film adopted Vertov as a cultural hero. Martin Scorsese, having picked up *Man with a Movie Camera* at random in a video store, professed himself thrilled by the possibilities it opened up. Vertov's semicoherent, ambiguous but deliriously confident experiments continue to astonish spectators and inspire filmmakers.

These three founding figures established three disparate sets of expectations among both filmmakers and viewers for documentary: ennobling entertainment (Flaherty), socially useful storytelling (Grierson), and provocative experiment (Vertov). Their names became synonymous with these approaches, and these three devolved into iconic figures for later documentarians.

Cinema Verité

Practices set in motion by the legendary trio of documentary founders were profoundly shaken up in the 1960s revolution that was variously called cinema verité, observational cinema, and direct cinema. This style broke dramatically with then-standard documentary practices of advance planning, scripting, staging, lighting, reenactment, and interviewing. All these traditional approaches had accommodated the limitations of large, heavy 35mm equipment, and they were appropriate to audience expectations of the time. Cinema verité (to use a popular umbrella term) employed the far lighter 16mm technology made more popular and accessible after the military deployed it during the war. Cinema verité spoke in a fresh voice, often about different subjects.

Cinema verité filmmakers took lighter, 16mm equipment into places that had not been seen before—the interiors of ordinary people's homes, on the dance floor with teenagers, back rooms in political campaigns, backstage with celebrities, on line with strikers, inside mental hospitals—and filmed what they saw. They took huge quantities of filmed footage into editing rooms, and through editing they found a story to tell. They used the innovation of sync (for "synchronized") sound—for the first time they could record image and sound simultaneously in 16mm— to overhear ordinary conversation, and they mostly did away with narration.

Practitioners now span the field, including filmmakers whose work antedates the movement, such as legendary French filmmaker Agnès Varda (*The Gleaners and I [Les Glaneurs et la glaneuse]*, 2000), filmmakers whose work shapes current practice such as Britain's Kim Longinotto, and China's Wang Bing (*West of Tracks [Tie Xi Qu]*, 2003), and emerging filmmakers. One demonstration of how commonly this style is picked up by aspiring filmmakers is the Steps for the Future project (2002). This international co-production between South African national television (SABC) and several European public service televisions tackled the controversial topic of AIDS in southern Africa. Some thirty-eight films resulted, most from first-time filmmakers; most were made using cinema verité conventions.

Evolution

This revolution in style began at a time of rising distrust among consumers of top-down media authority, perhaps seasoned by the public's experience of World War II propaganda and certainly by the rise of advertising as an international language of persuasion and the power of mass media. That distrust of media was itself imbedded in a much wider trend of social movements for justice, equality, political openness, and inclusion. These movements touched every corner of the world and resulted in the end of colonialism, changes in governments, and civil rights victories for discriminated-against social groups ranging from low-status castes to women to disabled people.

The first inklings of this movement in fact had nothing to do with technology. Films that emerged from Britain's Free Cinema movement in the late 1950s are distinguished by flouting the sober Griersonian mandate to educate and inform in the service of civic unity. Free Cinema literally freed itself from precisely that mandate. Lindsay Anderson's *O Dreamland* (1953) and Karel Reisz and Tony Richardson's *Momma Don't Allow* (1956) took viewers on a vacation with working-class kids going to an amusement part and a jazz club. The films did not implicitly judge their characters or dictate to viewers what to conclude from what they saw, nor did they tell viewers that what they were seeing was important. The films were chances to peer into zestful moments of ordinary life and frank statements about the personal interests of the filmmaker. Other work took a strong rebellious moral stance, opposed to the status quo. For example, French filmmaker Georges Franju made *Blood of the Beasts* (*Le sang des bêtes*, 1949) and *Hôtel des Invalides* (1952), profiling a slaughterhouse and a veterans' home, respectively. *Blood of the Beasts* exposed the cruelty behind the routine provisioning of meat and drew implicit comparisons between the slaughter of animals and that of people; the second was openly antimilitary and anticlerical.

Filmmakers in Canada, the United States, and France quickly pushed technological innovation to promote a new way of doing documentary. Time-Life Broadcasting bankrolled experiments by Robert Drew, who worked with engineer D A Pennebaker, and filmmakers David and Albert Maysles and Richard Leacock. (Leacock had become hooked on documentary by working with Flaherty on *Louisiana Story*.) With the help of French documentarian and engineer Jean-Pierre Beauviola, these innovative filmmakers succeeded in developing a system that recorded simultaneous sound without requiring all the equipment to be linked together and to the subject.

In the United States, experiments bloomed, not always successfully. The Drew team followed an electoral battle between John Kennedy and Hubert Humphrey in *Primary* (1960). Baffled ABC programmers refused to air it, saying it looked like "rushes" (the unedited day's footage); today, the film looks carefully crafted, although it communicates a breathless immediacy, as Jeanne Hall has stated. The ABC television network continued to dabble in the form, although it freely recut the material to fit the network's purposes. For instance, when Richard Leacock produced *Happy Mother's Day* (1963), a film about the birth of quintuplets that revealed crass commercialism in the public celebration of the births, ABC recut the footage to turn it into a heartwarming story of a town uniting to help the family. (Leacock later released the original.)

Cinema verité (sometimes called direct cinema, observational cinema, or in Canada, candid eye, after a TV series) electrified filmmakers with its possibilities. David and Al Maysles produced a series of striking feature documentaries that were celebrated in the arts-repertory circuit that was then a vital artery of film culture. In *Salesman* (1969), the brothers followed a group of Bible salesmen, who were living the contradictions of the American dream, as they relentlessly hawked a sacred book. Film editor Charlotte Zwerin turned their footage into an American tragedy. It was a sad and evocative statement about the collapse of a dream, which was released at the height of social divisions in the country around the Vietnam war and cultural values. Although *Salesman* had sharp social overtones, most of the Maysles's work avoided political subjects.

At the Canadian NFB, cinema verité—which began as a slap in the face of social moralism—became a central style, ironically for a unit started by John Grierson. One of the pioneer films was a portrait of teen idol Paul Anka, *Lonely Boy* (1961), which kicked off an entire category of backstage celebrity films. The NFB's Challenge for Change program—launched in 1966 by Colin Low and John

6. *Salesman*, a classic of cinema vérité filmmaking, turned the hawking of Bibles into a parable about the American dream. Directed by Albert Maysles and David Maysles, 1968.

Kemeny to encourage new voices and issues to surface in Canadian documentary, partly by training amateurs to use the camera—adopted cinema verité as its natural language. Grierson, always eager to show his influence, immediately claimed that Challenge for Change was only following in his tradition of documenting social problems.

Filmmakers worldwide seized upon the fly-on-the-wall opportunities provided by this approach. For instance, Nagisa Oshima produced for Japanese TV *The Forgotten Imperial Army* (1963), about Korean veterans of the Japanese army caught between Korea and Japan and without veterans' services. The renowned filmmaker Kon Ichikawa produced *Tokyo Olympiad* (1965), an ironic bow to German Leni Riefenstahl's exquisitely executed work for the Nazi government. Ichikawa closely observed athletes and made them not into emblems of the nation as Riefenstahl had, but into individuals struggling for their personal best. In India, the "parallel cinema" produced verité-style documentaries including S. Sukhdev's *India 67* (1967).

Inside institutions

Fred Wiseman, a Canadian lawyer-turned-filmmaker whose work was primarily done in the United States, produced work with a consistent, very different tone. His film career exposing the lived experience of institutions began with *Titicut Follies* (1967), which took viewers inside a Massachusetts mental hospital. A high school, hospital, boot camp, zoo, ballet company, court, housing project, and state legislature are among the many subjects of his films. They typically chronicle relationships that feature victims of impersonal, regimented social systems and the enforcers of those systems. The viewer never sees the filmmaker; there is no narration; the viewer simply enters the world of the institutionalized. And yet Wiseman, through sharply pointed editing and choices for subject matter, sits harshly in judgment on a system and society that treat human beings like problems to be managed. In *Titicut Follies*, it may have been this stern implicit indictment that led the Massachusetts state authorities to ban the film, even after it won awards; they argued that Wiseman had not gotten permission from enough people in the film to legally represent them on screen. The film may also have influenced the closing of the institution featured in the film. Wiseman's work has since been shown regularly on American public TV, where it has been an important demonstration of public TV's claim to innovation and significance.

To see how differently a participant-observation approach on institutions may be used, one might contrast *Titicut Follies*'s damning portrait with other films focusing on mental institutions. One of the best-known works of the Canadian documentarian Allan King, *Warrendale* (1967), let viewers spend time in a school for troubled young people. King's early hero had been Flaherty; King opposed the "propaganda" model of Grierson, which was so popular in Commonwealth countries. Grierson, he believed, had put the form into a "political straitjacket." *Warrendale*'s approach reflects his humanist outlook. Where Titicut is a place of horror, Warrendale—an experiment King admired—appears both prison and refuge, where suffering people undertake their own tentative recoveries with assistance. King portrayed Warrendale as an imperfect organism composed of flawed but mostly decent people.

Finally, one might look at *Thin* (2006), which shows an American clinic dealing with eating disorders. Directed by photographer Lauren Greenfield and produced by R. J. Cutler, a protégé of D A Pennebaker, the film takes viewers inside the clinic for a season, sharing with viewers the perspectives of both patients and staff. Rather than the judgment of Wiseman or the empathy of King, it brings voyeuristic fascination to its subject.

Provocation

Some filmmakers used the new techniques to provoke as well as to observe, as Erik Barnouw noted. In France, Jean Rouch, an anthropologist-filmmaker who wanted to let subjects tell their own stories, used new 16mm technology (in the process his team refined sync sound innovations) to probe the consciousness of postwar, postcolonial Paris. His group borrowed the term "cinema verité" from Dziga Vertov's *kino-pravda*, and they made *Chronicle of a Summer (Chronique d'un Été,* 1961).

The film records the interactions of a small group of young people, selected from co-director Edgar Morin's friends in a small, politically radical group. The friends conduct interviews with strangers on the street and film their own conversations. A Holocaust survivor's story shocks African students, who in turn expose the daily racism of the metropole toward the colonials; a neurotic Italian woman searches in vain for ordinary happiness. Within the film, characters comment on earlier parts of the film, and the filmmakers debate the different approaches.

The small experiment reverberated among activist-makers. The French radical director Chris Marker used its techniques to challenge the French with questions such as "Do you feel we live in a democracy?" in *The Lovely May* (1963); Jan Apta, a Czech filmmaker, conducted an on-camera survey of young people about their dreams and hopes in *Nejvetsi Prani* (*The Greatest Wish* [1964]); in *Opinião Publica* (*Public Opinion* [1967]), Brazilian filmmaker Arnaldo Jabor recorded the perspectives of lower-middle-class residents of Rio de Janeiro—a voice not heard before in Brazilian film and television.

Controversy

Cinema verité became a source of immense contention, partly because of the totalizing nature of its supporters' claims to truth. (Robert Drew blithely dismissed most previous documentaries with the simple word "fake.") In March 1963 at a film conference in Lyons, France, filmmakers debated the new approach. Enthusiasts decried the paternalistic and didactic model of Griersonian documentary, and celebrated the integrity and accuracy of cinema verité. Others resisted.

The Dutch activist filmmaker Joris Ivens resented the implicit claim in the term "cinema verité" that not only did it tell the truth but earlier forms of documentary did not. He followed that the claim skimmed over such important questions as "which truth and for whom? Seen by whom, and for whom?" The fantastic capacities of lightweight equipment also ran the risk, he said, "of skimming reality instead of penetrating it." And sometimes you needed to stop observing, he said, and "make militant films." The radical French director Jean-Luc Godard charged that cinema verité advocates had chosen to deny themselves the benefit of selection and reflection: "Deprived of consciousness, thus, Leacock's camera, despite its honesty, loses the two fundamental qualities of a camera: intelligence and sensibility."

Since then, debates have not stopped. Even the name for this approach has been contentious. Although Rouch had given cinema verité its name, he and other French filmmakers began calling their work "direct cinema." Meanwhile in the UK, where direct cinema had originated, cinema verité became a catchall term, as it did in the in the United States, for anything that involved no narration, a handheld camera, and the capture of action.

Some filmmakers reject the term, others the entire approach. "Cinema verité is the cinema of accountants," German filmmaker Werner Herzog told D A Pennebaker. Fred Wiseman called his films "reality fictions," arguing that he did not intend to represent reality objectively but to show *what* he saw and what he found interesting in that. Even this phrase was, he said, a "parody-pomposity term" invented to poke fun at the pretensions of cinema verité. The American documentarian Errol Morris inveighed against cinema verité, for claiming "that somehow if you juggle a camera around in your hands, sneak around in the corners of rooms and hide behind pillars, the Cartesian riddle will be solved as a result. That somehow epistemology will no longer play a role in what you do. That this is truth cinema, truth incarnate as revealed by a camera!" Lindsay Anderson, one of the pioneers of Free

Cinema, believed that direct cinema was "just an excuse for not being creative and being pretentiously journalistic."

Filmmakers who proudly call their work cinema verité still grapple with the question of what *kind* of truth cinema verité offers. Jean Rouch stated that the filmmaking process is "a sort of catalyst which allows us to reveal, with doubts, a fictional part of all of us, but which for me is the most real part of an individual." Canadian cinematographer and inventor Michel Brault neatly sidestepped the issue when he told critic Peter Wintonick, "You can't tell the truth—you can reveal." Canadian filmmaker Wolf Koenig (*Lonely Boy*) reverted to a familiar argument when he told Wintonick, "Every cut is a lie but you're telling a lie to tell the truth." These many twists of phrase recall the wry comment of theorist Noël Carroll: "Direct cinema opened a can of worms and then got eaten by them."

Critics have challenged the claim that filmmakers are showing unvarnished truth, even a subjective one. Jeanne Hall has shown how D A Pennebaker, in his pathbreaking verité portrait of Bob Dylan on tour, *Dont Look Back*, in fact carefully shaped the documentary to convey the filmmaker's own criticisms of the media. Thomas Benson and Carolyn Anderson charged that Fred Wiseman's films involve a contradiction, since he plays the role of author, and has created a work full of meaning but then withholds his meaning from the audience, thus demystifying institutions but mystifying his own role. A. William Bluem explored the possibility that the very spontaneity and emotionality of verité can obscure perception.

Others have pointed out that the approach can have effects opposite from the one that documentarians may hope for. Peter Davis's *Middletown* (1982), supposedly a summary of sociological research, ignored the research's conclusions in order to focus on crisis and peak moments in a season of the town's life. The cinema verité approach he chose, as Brian Winston mentioned, favored conflict in the day-to-day rather than the sociological insights of the report. After 1968, the French radical filmmaker and theorist Guy Hennebelle argued that some seemingly transparent practices—for instance, verité scenes of workers talking, which film activists believed might mobilize them for revolutionary action—could simply recapitulate the "false consciousness" of the workers themselves. "It is better to admit frankly the manipulation and make it agreeable to the eye and the ear by making use of the whole arsenal of the cinema," he declared.

The ethics of a verité filmmaker's relationship with the subject has often been raised. Filmmakers may inadvertently change the reality they film, and they may agonize over how much to intervene. The makers of Kartemquin Films's *Hoop Dreams* (1994), tracked two, poor, African American families over more than five years and sometimes contributed to family income; they believed modest contributions were part of a good-faith

7. Kartemquin Films used cinema verité to tell untold stories, including those of African American children (*Hoop Dreams*, 1994). Produced by Kartemquin Films.

relationship with the struggling families. The mother of the Loud family bemoaned that her family might never live down the publicity given to them in *An American Family* (1973), and indeed the Loud family continued to be targets of unwanted attention for decades. When the Maysles brothers filmed a concert of the Rolling Stones for the film that became *Gimme Shelter* (1970), the Hell's Angels were paid to keep order. But an altercation with a fan resulted in a death, which the film team captured on film, to some amount of criticism. Terry Zwigoff's *Crumb* (1995) exposed the private lives of the psychologically disturbed family of cartoonist R. Crumb for theatrical entertainment; Zwigoff had the consent of Crumb and his family, but some questioned the ability of the more disturbed family members to provide that consent.

Cinema verité is no longer revolutionary. It is the default language for music documentaries, and for all kinds of behind-the-scenes and the-making-of documentaries; it is part of the DNA of cop shows and docusoaps and part of the credibility apparatus of reality TV shows. It is built into expectations for grassroots video projects to expand expression, such as the BBC's *Video Diaries* project of the 1990s. The career of British filmmaker Nick Broomfield, whose sensationalist peerings into the lives of the famous and notorious are internationally successful, has depended on it. Cinema verité techniques are commonly used in political advertisements, to lend freshness and credibility. The approach has lost its novelty but not its ability to convince viewers that they are present, watching something unconstructed and uncontrovertibly real.

Chapter 2
Subgenres

We have established that documentary is a film genre in which a pledge is made to the viewer that what we will see and hear is about something real and true—and, frequently, important for us to understand. The filmmaker must, however, use a wide range of artifice in order to assert that claim, and many of them do their work in a commercial or semicommercial environment that constrains their choices. As documentary has evolved, so have standards, habits, conventions, and clichés around how filmmakers do their work.

We now turn to several subgenres to see how differently filmmakers have addressed the problems of representing reality within various subject areas.

Public Affairs

A good place to start looking at documentary's many subgenres is the public affairs documentary, which survives in the public television science series *Nova*, specials on such issues as poverty, government welfare programs, corporate corruption, and health care, and other public service programs. Such documentaries typically undertake an investigative or problem-oriented approach, feature sober exposition with narration and sometimes a host, make liberal use of background footage or b-roll, and focus on representative individuals as they exemplify or illustrate the problem. They promise an authoritative, often social-scientific view of an issue, speaking as professional journalists on behalf of a public affected by the problem.

This has been a socially influential and aesthetically durable form, which grew out of the early experiences of documentary makers and in the traditions of journalists. It is also the source of many viewers' expectations of objectivity and sobriety in documentary, and the reason why so many are surprised by the wide variety of work produced in the short history of documentary.

The broadcast TV public affairs documentary had its heyday from the mid-1950s to the mid-1980s, largely on commercial television. Major funders of public affairs documentaries were broadcasting companies, which produced these films in order to win prizes and prestige, to justify their use of airwaves they got licenses for from government, and as part of public service mandates explicitly imposed by regulators. As television became the primary vehicle by which people learned about the world beyond their own experience, the power of television broadcasters to affect public opinion—and therefore elite decision making—grew. And as it expanded, broadcast executives became ever-more implicated in elite politics.

Public affairs documentaries evolved as a more seasoned, thoughtful version of news—a kind of feature magazine to the news' headlines. For Fred Friendly, the legendary producer who worked with Edward R. Murrow and later became a leader of public television, the job was "interpretation, background and understanding at a time when comprehension is falling behind the onrush of events." The men and (much less frequently) women who produced these documentaries saw themselves as journalists, often investigative journalists. They believed in the role of journalism as a Fourth Estate: a watchdog on power. At the same time, cautious executive producers needed high ratings to survive and were acutely aware of close scrutiny by powerful politicians, who held the ability to revoke licenses and mandates.

History and culture

The advent of television in the 1950s dramatically changed the opportunities and challenges for documentarians. Early documentaries had been made by filmmakers; now people flooded into television from radio and print journalism. The BBC launched *Special Enquiry* (1952–57) and *Panorama*, which continues. Granada TV, a British commercial channel, launched *World in Action* (1963–98). In the United States, the three networks each had series: CBS's *See It Now* (1951–58), followed in 1959 by *CBS Reports*, and NBC's *White Paper*, followed later by ABC's *Close-Up!* (1960–63). The Australian Broadcasting Corporation launched *Chequerboard* (1970–72), and *Four Corners*, which is still running. Because they were produced in series through major news and information outlets, such public affairs documentaries implicitly asserted that the topics they covered were the most important topics of the day.

The public affairs documentary series has been threatened by nearly every business development in television. Growing audiences raised the ratings stakes, and competition from the advent of multichannel cable television, satellites, and the Internet made it ever-harder to justify high budgets. Deregulation and privatization vastly reduced public interest obligations. In the 1970s and 1980s, U.S. networks dropped series and turned to specials, sometimes outsourcing them to freelancers ranging from Hollywood-centric David Wolper to scruffy independent Jon Alpert.

The 1970s also saw the rise of newsmagazines, such as *60 Minutes* and *20/20*. These highly formatted shows further undercut television public affairs documentary, while drawing on their prestige. Producer Tom Spain, who started out working on

Twentieth Century under Richard Paley's CBS, believed that the "good days"—what others called the "golden age"—ended "when *60 Minutes* started to make money...we thought of ourselves as, maybe, Mr. Paley's kennel full of well-bred dogs—he could show us off, have us do tricks, and be a kind of loss leader." By the 1990s, public affairs documentary on the "golden age" model was a rarity on commercial television everywhere. Public service television continued to produce high-end public affairs documentaries, but producers also began searching for ways to make significant work on much lower budgets and with different models. For instance, in the United States the public affairs series *Frontline*, always an innovator, continued to produce its prestigious programs and also experimented with low-budget programs, sometimes showcased on the World Wide Web, produced with the latest digital equipment.

Public TV

Public television in the United States was born, in part, out of the frustration of large foundation executives with the limits of public affairs documentary on commercial television. The Ford Foundation bankrolled an effort that found traction in the White House; by 1967 an entity had been created to channel federal funds (never to become more than a fifth of public television's funding, however) to hundreds of local stations throughout the country. The foundation funded controversial documentaries, including *Banks and the Poor* (1970), which criticized bank lending policies that excluded whole neighborhoods. One of the lenders criticized was a major donor to Richard Nixon's presidential campaign. Nixon waged war on public affairs on public television and was stopped only by impeachment.

The experience left station managers leery of all public affairs. Foundations funded documentarians who could negotiate the anxieties of the Public Broadcasting Service and its member stations. Expert journalists such as Bill Moyers, Roger Weisberg, Hedrick Smith, and Alvin Perlmutter executed heavily researched and highly professional works on large topics such as education, gentrification, and even death and dying. Investigative journalism on timely political topics was more controversial and even harder to fund.

As cheaper production fueled a dissident generation in the 1970s, independent producers organized to insist on space on public television. Series such as *Frontline*, which featured investigative journalism, and *P.O.V.*, which showcased work in a personal voice, resulted. In 1991, independent producers eventually succeeded in dedicating federal funds within public television for the Independent Television Service, which largely produces documentaries.

Influence and significance

Network public affairs documentaries often have attracted enormous attention. Intense controversy circulated around the several episodes of *See It Now* in which Edward R. Murrow challenged the antidemocratic intimidation of Communist witch hunts, and he finally took on Sen. Joseph McCarthy, one of the most publicity-hogging of the witch-hunters. (The 2005 feature film *Good Night, and Good Luck* draws on this history.) The 1968 *CBS Reports* program "Hunger in America" exposed the failures of the federal welfare system and generated so much public reaction that the Senate held a hearing and funds for the programs were increased. *The Defense of the United States* (1980), a terrifying CBS documentary on U.S. nuclear military policy, was widely seen in Europe and may have soured European governments on U.S. military plans. The work of British filmmaker Adrian Cowell for British commercial television on Brazilian rainforest devastation—the *Decade of Destruction* series (1980–90)—informed a successful campaign by nongovernmental organizations to reform World Bank environmental policies. The BBC documentary *The Power of Nightmares* (2004) by Adam Curtis, which argued that the rise of Muslim fundamentalists had been aided by neoconservative zealots in the United States, raised an international uproar.

At the same time, broadcasters have often avoided being on the bleeding edge of an issue. Ed Murrow waited a full two years, for example, before he took on McCarthy. The BBC hesitated to show *The Power of Nightmares* and initially aired it without publicity. Until the later 1960s, the U.S. networks studiously avoided the Vietnam War; they also avoided any recognition of documentaries done around the world, including in Cuba and Vietnam, on the subject. Several Canadian documentaries by internationally renowned broadcast journalists such as Michael Maclear and Beryl Fox were not shown in the United States, presumably because executives chose not to ruffle politicians' feathers or because they themselves participated in the same social circles and internalized the political elite's distaste for dissent.

CBS's *Morley Safer's Vietnam* (1967) finally broke the silence, with uncommented but damning footage showing a war far different from the one represented by the government, and this film seemed to open up possibility. CBS commissioned the British journalist Felix Greene to make a film about North Vietnam, but the network then apparently lost courage and canceled the contract. However, the new public broadcasting service picked up the show. Greene's *Inside North Vietnam* (1968) showed a determined, even happy people, whose nationalist ambitions reminded some reviewers of American colonists' aspirations. The film outraged some congressional representatives, one of whom threatened to cut funding for public television.

As antiwar protest and public opinion grew, U.S. networks gathered more courage. In 1971 CBS aired *The Selling of the Pentagon*, sometimes regarded as the apex of this kind of public affairs documentary. It revealed the extent of the U.S. military's public relations machinery and even criticized the network's own (occasional) complicity. The airing drew so much attention—including outrage from the administration and the Pentagon—that a second broadcast drew higher ratings than the first. The

Pentagon withdrew some of the public relations materials criticized in the reporting.

Independent filmmakers meanwhile made very different work, which was not broadcast. Their work often eschewed the soberly objective stance and claim to comprehensiveness of broadcast documentaries. Antiwar activists used Michael Rubbo's Canadian documentary *Sad Song of Yellow Skin* (1969), in which the small crew followed three U.S. journalists around Saigon, to mobilize support for their cause. Emile de Antonio created an analytic history of the Vietnam War as a continuation of imperialist policy in *In the Year of the Pig* (1968), which was shown in theaters. In 1974 Peter Davis, who had produced *The Selling of the Pentagon*, made *Hearts and Minds*, a pointed, heartbreaking document showing what Davis believed was the betrayal of fundamental U.S. beliefs and ideals in the Vietnam War. Where the CBS film had been a tough and damning piece of reporting, *Hearts and Minds* was an expression of grief and rage.

Conventions and criticisms

The differences in style and tone between *Selling* and *Hearts* speak to the conventions of public affairs documentaries. Network documentaries were highly crafted, institutional products. They were professionally produced, using lighting, editing, and scripting techniques drawn from Hollywood filmmaking. The personalities, and sometimes even the names, of the producers who were responsible for them were absorbed into the broadcast network's institutional identity, represented by the host.

The producers developed a range of conventions to communicate authority, accessibility, balance, accuracy, and significance. They usually used an interviewer/host who could register both authority and accessibility. Ed Murrow was a model, with his rolled-up sleeves, cigarette, and somber tones, surrounded by TV equipment and the aura that his radio reputation cast. His demeanor communicated knowledge without elitism. The programs used plenty of b-roll and symbolic material, and as the tempo of TV picked up they began to use interview footage as story elements, clipping out remarks and inserting them into the story line. Sound was king; both narration and soundtrack led the viewer through the analysis.

Thus, it was a shock to U.S. network executives when *Life* photographer Robert Drew and his team in 1959 proposed to ABC an entirely different way of making public affairs documentaries. Using more lightweight, mobile equipment, capturing events rather than interviews, they promised viewers a fly-on-the-wall individual experience rather than an institutional analysis. Programmers tried it, with grave doubts. Gradually, cinema verité influences appeared in network public affairs, without overthrowing the crafted-and-narrated approach. The BBC and Canadian Broadcasting Corporation also tried out observational public affairs documentaries, also without abandoning the analytically crafted model. New formats appeared. In 1964 the British commercial channel Granada TV daringly aired *Seven Up*, the beginning of a series in which children of different socioeconomic status in the same classroom were followed at seven-year intervals throughout their lives. The series contained elements both of observation and concern for grassroots experience of verité and the narration, interview, and problem-orientation of the established public affairs documentary.

Network public affairs documentaries in the pre-cable era were highly influential, but they also opened wounds. In rural Appalachia, which was the focus of several network documentaries on poverty and inequality, many resented becoming "poverty" poster children and believed their cultural values had been slighted. At the same time a regional arts center, Appalshop, had been started with federal funds from Lyndon Johnson's Great Society initiative. Documentaries exploring the hill culture of the region became its priority. *Stranger with a Camera* (2000), made by one of the Appalshop founders, Elizabeth Barret, reveals the long-term ethical reverberations for locals and mediamakers; the film highlights a 1967 incident when a cantankerous landowner, angry at media outsiders, shot a liberal Canadian photo-journalist associated with television public affairs.

The network television documentary has been examined more by journalists and journalism scholars than by cinema studies scholars. (This might be in part because the subgenre's corporate identity complicates the director-focused, auteurist approach of many film scholars.) The Australian independent broadcast journalist John Pilger argued passionately that the much-vaunted impartiality of traditional TV documentary "is the expression of a middle-class consensus politics" that privileges power. Instead, he proposed, journalists should vigorously be watchdogs on power and defenders of the public interest. The conventions of public affairs broadcast journalism have been analyzed by communications scholars. Thomas Rosteck has shown how *See It Now*'s McCarthy coverage was cannily constructed to prejudice the Senator while seeming to be balanced and objective. Richard Campbell analyzed the format of the newsmagazines that provided a shrunken version of public affairs documentaries' mission, noting that *60 Minutes* episodes are structured like detective stories. The newsmagazines thus cannot tackle issues that fall outside the detective story model and cannot be resolved by "finding the villain." Most social problems, from global warming to traffic jams, are in general not the fault of one bad guy.

The public affairs documentary has lost its most munificent patrons, the old-style commercial network and national broadcasters; both face brutal competition that lowers budgets. The role of the authoritative broadcast journalist is also coming into question. Still, the style of the crafted, narrated, hosted documentary, positing an important concern to be investigated and understood and featuring a well-known, trustworthy host, remains a sturdy model. It continues to be a default choice in broadcast journalism worldwide, and it is also often imitated in work produced by and for nonprofit organizations striving for legitimacy and authority on any specific topic.

Government Propaganda

At the other end of the spectrum from the claims of public affairs documentary, which rests for authority on its journalistic expertise, is government propaganda—an important source of funding and training for documentarians worldwide and sometimes a powerful influence on public opinion.

Propaganda documentaries are made to convince viewers of an organization's point of view or cause. These films peddle the convictions not of the filmmaker but of the organization, although some makers fully support the cause. Although such work might be generated by anyone, including advertisers and activists, the term "propaganda" is more often connoted with governments. Documentaries have been valuable to governments precisely because of their claims to truthfulness and fidelity to real life. The height of importance for propaganda documentary was in the period before, during, and immediately after World War II, when film was the dominant audio-visual medium.

Documentaries were used by governments to influence public opinion from the origins of film. As warfare moved to the model of "total war" in World War I, governments used media to motivate their own troops, mobilize their own civilians, and convince others of their might. The British documentary *The Battle of the Somme* (1916), which succeeded with British audiences in theaters largely because it showed actual battle footage, is a well-known example.

After World War I, governments worldwide saw documentary as a new and potent tool. The Nazi party in Germany, rising to power in 1933, consolidated control over production, distribution, and exhibition of all films. Its political legitimacy was directly fed by propaganda. In Japan, the government in 1939 passed a law requiring filmmakers to hew to the government line and required theaters to show documentaries in every film program. The following year, the government forced a merger of leading news film companies to foster conformity of message in order to promote uniformity of behavior. The nascent Soviet government nationalized all media, in service of state agendas. The 1920s saw tremendous artistic ferment, as Dziga Vertov's career showed, followed by collapse into grim Stalinist socialist realism.

Propaganda agencies were created in Britain and the United States, but they had to negotiate with commercial producers, distributors, and exhibitors to get messages to their own citizens, except for members of the armed forces. Britain created a Ministry of Information, which was riddled with contradictory policies from the start. The U.S. Office of War Information was never fully supported by President Roosevelt, and each wing of the armed forces controlled its own propaganda production. American propaganda production also ran into opposition from Hollywood, where studios checked every attempt to create government products that might infringe upon business.

In Britain, Grierson's teams created some of critics' most treasured and troubling documentaries. Basil Wright's *Song of Ceylon* (1934) is an excellent example. It not only romanticized precolonial life in one of Britain's key tea-producing areas but also celebrated the impressive industrial process by which tea arrived at Britons' kitchens. It thus glamorized tea drinking, as William Guynn has noted, making the act a participation in a nostalgic view of an exotic culture, while also celebrating the energy and power of Britain.

Roosevelt's New Deal ameliorated economic crisis with shocking new government investment—and intrusion—into the lives of citizens, a change that called for persuasion. Different agencies employed documentarians, often drawing from the pool of radicalized artists who had been producing activist documentaries. The biggest of these was the Resettlement Administration, where writer and analyst Pare Lorentz became the producer of several celebrated documentaries.

Lorentz strove to make works of art in the service of state objectives he profoundly believed in, as did Grierson in Britain and Vertov in the Soviet Union. His projects showed the influence of European and Soviet artists' debates. They used sound as an independent element, not merely for background; they created associations through visual and auditory poetry; they echoed the look of city symphonies. Each of the Lorentz films negotiated between the often-radical analyses of filmmakers and official directives. William Alexander stated that Lorentz softened social analysis, particularly finger-pointing at greedy capitalists.

The Plow that Broke the Plains (1936), charged with encouraging public support for relief programs of the Resettlement Administration (later the Farm Security Administration), was a rueful look backward at the process by which people's choices had destroyed the ecology of the central plains and resulted in mass migration. Hollywood businesses refused to share footage with Lorentz, and major distributors refused to carry the film in their theaters, but independent theaters turned it into a minor hit. *The River* (1937) poetically argued the need for government intervention in water management and conservation by looking at the destructive power of the Mississippi; Lorentz sometimes called it an "opera." Paramount distributed it and actually made money, but studios remained hostile to government filmmaking.

The films that Lorentz made or supervised became classics among film students for their bold artistic experiment. They retain fascination for historians because they capture a moment when governments worldwide were—for good or ill—suddenly taking on enormous social and physical engineering projects.

Different goals, different styles

A comparison of three government propaganda documentaries shows how propaganda differs according to the government mandate and the cultural context as well as the artist. Three filmmakers chose three different stylistic approaches to the challenge of shaping viewers' ideology with reality.

The German filmmaker Leni Riefenstahl's *Triumph of the Will* (1935) was an excellent exemplification of the goal of Nazi film propaganda: to conflate Hitler with the nation, and to represent the party and later the state as a totalized, unified, and irresistible force. Documentaries were only one of a wide range of symbolic tools to achieve that aim. That symbolic power, which Riefenstahl employed so well, was intended to impress supporters and intimidate others, including foreign enemies.

Made to document the 1934 rally of the Nazi party and funded by the German national studio UFA, *Triumph of the Will* is a spectacularly choreographed representation of an already spectacularly choreographed event. It visually deifies Hitler—the opening scene shows him arriving from the clouds. It represents the German people as a highly disciplined, worshipful mass, acting with one purpose: to serve Hitler as an equivalent of the nation. With its shots of euphoric faces idolizing Hitler, telescoped crowd scenes inspiring awe, swelling orgasmic music, and shots of individuals young and old all sharing the same actions and emotions, the film makes political union, as Frank Tomasulo noted, positively sexy. Although it chronicles a political rally, the film carefully steers clear of political debate. The film is about the emotional thrill of belonging, of being part of something grandly historic.

As World War II began, the British had an entirely different challenge from that of the Germans. The "People's War" would be won by a mobilized population, but the nation had almost lost the war in the first attack. Britons needed confidence in their own abilities to resist. British propaganda, after a rocky and preachy start and heavy censorship, developed a reputation for honesty and truth-telling—giving Britons the real facts, real battle scenes, real war news, and real people.

Grierson's teams made dozens of documentaries. Perhaps the film that best exemplifies the British propaganda approach of celebrating ordinary people's ability to maintain their culture under pressure is *Listen to Britain* (1942) by Humphrey Jennings. An upper-class artist, he created several well-known wartime documentaries, all of them marked by a fascination with small but telling detail. He worked in *Listen to Britain*, as he did in others, with the brilliant editor Stewart McAllister.

Listen to Britain is a visual poem, seen through glimpses of everyday moments in a Britain on constant guard for planes and bombs. The viewer seemingly overhears the continuing sounds of daily life—children dancing in a courtyard, a chorus of a traditional song by ambulance workers, an upper-class recital, an American GI teaching "Home on the Range" to his Allied colleagues—as the camera wanders through streets and peers into rooms. Briefcase-laden men pick their way through rubble-strewn, bombed streets on their way to work; women take on surveillance duties uncomplainingly.

Some have argued that Jennings cynically played upon the myth that a class-riven Britain happily united around the war challenge, and others have said rather that he subtly pointed up the realities of class tensions in his contrasting images. However you read the work, Jennings produced a highly popular, short film that evoked a shared understanding among Britons that they would uncomplainingly do what it took to win, without giving up who they were. His approach was appropriate to the kind of message he wanted to deliver. His disarming method was to appear not to be propagandizing at all.

The United States faced still different challenges. The federal government had no freestanding propaganda ministry or documentary production unit. The Americans entered the war belatedly, and many people in the United States resisted support for the Allies until the Japanese bombing of Pearl Harbor. Moreover, young men who were mobilized for the armed forces often came from farms or small towns and had shallow educations; they had no idea why they were supposed to risk their lives.

The hallmark work of U.S. war propaganda was the *Why We Fight* (1943) series, produced by noted Hollywood director (and Sicilian immigrant) Frank Capra for the Army's Information and Education division. It addressed both isolationists and the ignorant. Commissioned by the U.S. Army, the eight-part series was designed to explain to American troops why the country was involved in this war. Capra drew on the film work of the U.S. Signal Corps, and he freely used his Hollywood connections. The key to his project, though, was the work of other nations' propagandists—especially the work of Riefenstahl. He interwove images from Hollywood films (after overcoming studio resistance), animated maps from the Disney studios, U.S. Army footage, and enemy propaganda turned into a portrayal of danger. Riefenstahl's ability to overwhelm the German viewer was, reinvented through American eyes, a sound to alarm.

The *Why We Fight* series is a set of didactic, emotionally powerful arguments for U.S. involvement in the war. The style is jaunty, confident, even brash, drawing on the American popular culture of newspapers, radio, and film that was then the staple media diet of young Americans. Political arguments are simplified, sometimes into falsity. No mention of segregation, for instance, creeps into the rosy portrait of American democracy. Capra brought his trademark populist sentiment for "the American way of life" to the project. The contemporary political crisis was put in the context of American populist and democratic values meshed with the quality of small-town, neighborhood life. He had little control over the overt political messages, which were set by military officers.

These three filmmakers used radically different styles—dazzling spectacle, deliberate understatement, forthright direct address. Their work reflects distinct cultural contexts as well as political missions. The filmmakers shared, however, a core strategy: to link the present crisis to what viewers could see as their enduring values and cultural heritage.

Effectiveness

Are propaganda documentaries effective? Nicholas Reeves, drawing on rich literature on media effects, has concluded that these films, like the propaganda efforts of governments generally, succeeded where they were able to reinforce beliefs—propaganda films have never been very effective at changing public opinion. Claims for the power of any one piece of propaganda to poison or control the minds of viewers seem universally to be overstated. At the same time, each documentary forms part of a larger picture of persuasion and agenda-setting, creating expectations and gradually redrawing mental maps of what is normal.

Propaganda films also have lacked the appeal of commercial fiction films. During World War II, propaganda films were more often shown in nontheatrical screenings than in theaters. In Japan, where documentaries were mandated, wartime studies showed that the documentaries attracted relatively few women. In Germany *Triumph of the Will*, despite the Hitlerian state's unsubtle promotion of it to theater owners, often ran for only one week in theaters because of small audiences. The film did not seem to improve public opinion soured by bad economic news and alarm over Nazi anti-Semitic extremism. The achievement of *Triumph of the Will* may have been at a deeper level not reflected in polls; it associated the newcomer Nazis with deep cultural and historical traditions.

8. *Triumph of the Will* provided propaganda not only for the Nazis but also, when recut, for the Allies. Directed by Leni Riefenstahl, 1935.

In Britain, "people's war"–themed documentaries lasted longer in theaters than more timely and preachy propaganda. Humphrey Jennings's 1940 *London Can Take It* was the first box office success. It featured an American journalist's reporting, with the underlying motif that Germans cannot "kill the unconquerable spirit and courage of the people of London." *Listen to Britain* was another audience success, but it was an exception. Documentaries were also taken on the road, with 16mm projectors for organized screenings.

In the United States, Capra's series was shown to just about every soldier at home and abroad. Studies showed that the films affected soldiers' opinions both immediately after viewing and later. With their uncomplicated celebration of the Allies, the films were also popular with British and Russian governments, which ordered them shown in theaters. The series was less successful in U.S. theaters. Theater owners did not want to show the *Why We Fight* series, in part because of bad experiences with documentaries, and in part because the series reused much material—especially newsreels—that had already been shown in theaters.

Viewers do not surrender easily to propaganda they can identify. *Triumph of the Will* could be used by so many for counterpropaganda so effectively because its command over the viewer is imperial; it became a visual demonstration of the will to conquer and crush. One of the reasons *Listen to Britain* has remained so beloved is because it creates the impression among viewers that it is not attempting to control their minds but inviting them in to observe a reality.

Results of a propaganda film can be far different from expected, as the reuse of Riefenstahl's work has shown. The American Hollywood director John Huston made a wartime film for the American armed forces, *The Battle of San Pietro* (1945), to inform Americans of the need for the high-casualty fighting in Italy. Because it was so graphic, the government chose not to use his film during the war for fear of alarming the populace, although it reversed its decision after the war's end. The film, with its unique battle photography, has been used since by antiwar activists, among others, to demonstrate the high human cost of war.

The work of Akira Iwasaki, as recalled by Erik Barnouw, is an ironic tale of propaganda redeployed and suppressed. Having been forced to work as a filmmaker for the Japanese government during World War II, Iwasaki had the equipment and skills to record the aftermath of the bombing of Hiroshima and Nagasaki. The U.S. occupation government, however, soon confiscated and classified his work. When the work was declassified, Erik Barnouw produced a short, powerfully moving film, *Hiroshima-Nagasaki, August 1945*. When Iwasaki saw the film, he saw his own footage on the screen for the first time.

Ethics

If documentary pledges to show viewers a good-faith representation of reality, can an honest filmmaker produce propaganda and really call it a documentary? Many broadcast journalists would regard it as career-destroying to take a government contract. Independent filmmakers likewise prize their autonomy from government dictates and censorship. At the same time, many film production companies make their bread and butter producing training and promotional documentaries for governments, although this is generally regarded as unglamorous work.

Filmmakers in the World War II era often believed they had not only a right but an obligation to produce propaganda. John Grierson thought that intellectuals had an obligation to work for a strong and unified but still open society. As he explained at the time, "Simply put, *propaganda is education*. The 'manipulation' in our films combines aesthetics with ideas of democratic reform. We are medicine men hired to mastermind. We are giving every individual a living conception of the community which he has the privilege to serve." Compromise was both a harsh reality and a privilege. "The first rule of filmmaking is don't pistol-whip the hand that holds the wallet," he once said about the absence of class conflicts in his government projects.

Frank Capra saw no contradiction in working for the U.S. Army, although he was often exasperated by the difficulties and frustrated by conflicting demands from military authorities. Capra proudly put his talents in the service of fighting fascism as did other leading Hollywood talents, some of whom had left-wing political beliefs and who saw fascism as the primary threat to a more socially just future. After the war, scriptwriter Budd Schulberg produced a series of documentaries promoting the Marshall Plan for European consumption.

On the other hand and on the losing side, Leni Riefenstahl, who spent four years in a de-Nazification program after World War II, found that her association with Hitler tainted her for the rest of her life. She tried to argue that she was simply making art, not propaganda, but that she was forced to make propaganda. Until she died at the age of 101 in 2003, she insisted that she had never been a Nazi, that she had little option but to work for Hitler, and that she merely produced the most beautiful work she could under the circumstances.

Legacy

Propaganda, also known as disinformation, public diplomacy, and strategic communication, continues to be an important tool for governments. But stand-alone documentary is no longer an important part of public relations campaigns aimed at the general public. Government propaganda has been the object of attention by documentarians, though, as in the broadcast public affairs documentary *The Selling of the Pentagon*, Jayne Loader and Kevin and Pierce Rafferty's *The Atomic Café* (1982), which is a sardonic look at government propaganda about the nuclear age, and Robert Stone's *Radio Bikini* (1987) about the extraordinary U.S. government public relations campaign around the first H-bomb explosion.

Government propaganda organizations started in wartime have blossomed in peacetime. The National Film Board of Canada began as a wartime endeavor. Japanese government support for World War II propaganda films greatly expanded the capacity of the industry, and readied it for postwar, privately capitalized production.

One generation's propaganda is another's treasure trove. Deep archives of newsreels, documentary, training, and other actuality footage became a resource for later compilation films and TV series. For example, the American network TV series *Victory at Sea* (1952–53) drew heavily on navy filming. World War II–themed documentaries on cable channels have depended on public domain, government footage from World War II. Private businesses have flourished by cataloguing and indexing U.S. government materials. The Prelinger Archives also makes government films available in a free, downloadable digital form off the Internet.

Although documentary films are no longer primary vehicles for government propaganda, governments continue to invest in film and video for a very different purpose: surveillance. This ubiquitous practice can become fodder for documentarians as well. In Eastern Europe, after the fall of the Berlin wall in 1989, government archives became raw material for documentary films reexamining history. In the Polish filmmaker Piotr Morawski's *The Secret Tapes* (2002), secret police filmmakers recalled their jobs, voicing over footage from an accidentally abandoned carton of film. The film's sly humor comes from the filmmakers' evident nostalgia for their former jobs. Peruvian intelligence minister Vladimiro Montesinos's records of his illegal bribes were ultimately shown on television and resulted in Sonia Goldenberg's acidic documentary *Eye Spy* (2002).

Propaganda documentaries put a spotlight on the problems of representing reality built into the documentary genre. They use the same techniques as documentaries made for any other purpose. Like other documentaries, they are designed to show the viewer something the viewer can believe is true; the realities they show fit into an ideological context that gives the films meaning. They are not necessarily made in bad faith. Indeed, often the makers are patriots who see themselves contributing to the public good with their skills. They might even be truthful, or at least show a reality that the filmmaker believes to be true.

Propaganda documentaries differ from other documentaries in their backers, who are agents of the state—the social institution that sets and enforces the rules of society, ultimately through force. Those backers control the message. Those differences ramify the significance of propaganda documentaries, since the portrayal of reality is backed by such enormous power. These documentaries dramatically demonstrate that no documentary is a transparent window onto reality, and that all meaning-making is motivated. They also remind us of the importance of examining the conditions of production of any cultural expression.

Advocacy

Documentaries produced for political causes, by advocates and activists, raise similar issues as government propaganda documentaries, but they operate in a different context.

What distinguishes an advocacy film like one in the American Civil Liberties Union's Freedom Files or in the Sierra Club Chronicles (both at aclu.tv) from propaganda like Frank Capra's wartime work? Both of them are created by producers for organizations in order to promote the agenda of the organization. The big difference is in the nature of the sponsoring organizations. The state wields a unique power and authority over its citizens; its persuasion is often a tool in its repressive apparatus.

By contrast, in an open society civil society organizations' promotion of their own perspectives (with a few exceptions such as treason and obscenity) is regarded as contributing to a vital public sphere. The greater the activity of a wide range of civil society organizations in expressing their perspectives and appealing to a public to engage with them, the healthier a society is seen to be. American law in particular is anchored in the First Amendment, which endorses the idea that, as Supreme Court Justice Louis Brandeis put it, the remedy for bad speech is more speech.

What distinguishes an advocacy film like *Celsius 41.11*, produced by the American conservative advocacy group Citizens United, from a passionately argued independent film like *Fahrenheit 9/11*, to which it responds? The answer: Both its affiliation with an organization and its focus on supporting the organization's work with instrumental action by viewers. You may agree or disagree with Michael Moore, but he is one person, albeit a celebrity. Moore's arguments inspire conversation and may lead some viewers to express their disagreement with foreign policy (and others to rail at Michael Moore and liberals). They are direct interventions in public conversation. By contrast, advocacy films are tools of an organization's mobilization for action on specific issues or causes.

Advocates and activists have often chosen documentary because it is a relatively low-budget way to counter the status quo as expressed in mainstream media. They have grappled with questions of subject and form in their search for the most effective way to reach viewers. Advocacy films are usually highly focused and designed to motivate viewers to a particular action. Like government propaganda films, they may be made in good faith by people who profoundly agree with an organization's agenda. They, like propaganda films, deserve attention from anyone who wants to understand the techniques of persuasion—and nothing persuades like reality.

"Committed"

In the tumultuous 1930s, when the Great Depression thoroughly shook the faith of many in the future of capitalism, many left-wing political groups and many of the film clubs populated by fashionably left-wing young people saw documentary film as a tool to challenge the status quo. They wanted to make "committed" films—supportive of social and even revolutionary change.

In continental Europe, the UK, Japan, and the United States, enthusiastic young people debated the latest work of Vertov,

Eisenstein, Flaherty, and the Grierson teams in cinema clubs around the globe. Inspired by Vertov's Kino-Eye newsreel work, they made newsreels that countered the popular and often right-wing newsreels shown in theaters. In the United States, the Film and Photo League created a widely seen series of worker-oriented newsreels featuring strikes and demonstrations. These were simple records of events, photographed with a sympathetic eye for workers. Filmmakers showed the newsreels to each other, to recruits, and to political groups and rallies.

These political parties and cinema clubs were incubators for documentarians. The filmmakers who went to work for Pare Lorentz in the Roosevelt Administration began there, and so did Dutch activist filmmaker Joris Ivens. The stridency of the work is exemplified by a short film Ivens made with Belgian cinema club leader Henri Storck, *Borinage* (1933), portraying the miners as cruelly plunged into poverty as a result of a classic capitalist crisis of overproduction. "We wanted to shout our indignation by using the starkest images possible," said Storck later. The film, a didactic and angry indictment, used reenactment and condemnatory juxtaposition.

As the Great Depression deepened, in many countries the Communist Party (CP), affiliated with the Soviet Union, gained credibility. The CP had a powerful influence on progressive politics internationally, and on cultural work associated with it, including film. For instance, many of the Film and Photo League filmmakers were CP members, and the organization was informally part of the CP's "cultural front."

The connection with the Communist Party was crucial; it created community, it allowed people to pool resources, it provided audiences, and it shaped messages. The Spanish civil war provides one good example. The civil war broke out in 1936 when some military officers revolted against the Nazi-allied Franco government. The anti-Franco or Republican movement grew; the

CP dominated, with the help of the USSR. CP leaders brutally suppressed other political factions, including anarchists. Internationally, some saw the war as an antifascist struggle requiring international solidarity, while others saw it as a national issue in which they should not meddle and resisted supporting the CP.

Internationally, filmmakers rallied to make films about the war, in order to raise awareness and funds for the anti-Franco forces. These films glossed over internal factionalism and encouraged international support for the Republicans, as suited the CP. One of the best known is *The Spanish Earth* (1937). The film was made by an international team—Ivens as director, Helen van Dongen as editor, with script and narration by Ernest Hemingway—for Hollywood backers. It demonstrates an artful approach to political truth telling and incidentally shows the growing aesthetic versatility of Ivens—who went on to become a leading activist filmmaker and mentor for many others, until his death in 1989.

In an approach that evokes the romantic realism of Robert Flaherty, the film brings viewers into the daily life of a village near Madrid. Filmed in the midst of the war, it documents the building of an irrigation canal crucial to crops that would feed embattled Madrid. The film's focus on the rhythms of daily life invites the viewer into the work and habits of the villagers. Now we see that the war is also part of the villagers' daily lives; we see them slinging guns, standing guard, surveying the wreckage after a bomb attack. The villagers' unstinting support for the anti-Franco cause is woven into the values and fabric of everyday life.

Ivens, with the help of Hemingway's spare narration, managed to sidestep messy political questions about factional conflict. The film communicated human warmth rather than delivering political information; Ivens used the techniques of realism to bring viewers' feelings to the fore. Although the film had only a modest theatrical run, it raised a substantial amount of money for the anti-Franco

Republicans in its screenings, both in theaters and in cinema clubs as well as in private showings.

The Spanish Earth also demonstrated one response to a debate common among activist filmmakers at the time: should one make "militant" films to mobilize one's own constituency to act, or should one be reaching out to convince broader audiences of a point of view? This second resort would require more artfulness, which *The Spanish Earth* successfully employed. The New York filmmakers who established the filmmaking group Nykino after a political and aesthetic split with the Film and Photo League also took up the second approach in making another famous advocacy film of the time, *Native Land* (1942). Using dramatic reenactments, the film drew upon a congressional investigation of civil liberties violations, and strove to inspire a greater demand for social justice and fair and equal treatment under the law. The film could not compete with Hollywood's production values, though, and by 1942 its message had been overtaken by wartime patriotism.

The advent of World War II put an end to many experiments in committed filmmaking. In Germany and Japan, governments ruthlessly suppressed cinema clubs. The combination of anti-communist witch-hunting and the self-discrediting of Soviet communism after the 1956 revelations of the horrors of Stalinism and the Soviet invasion of Hungary distanced many intellectuals and artists from CP politics.

"Third cinema"

In the 1960s civil rights and human rights movements, struggles against colonialism, nuclear weapons, and the Cold War arms race all marked a time of political ferment. The technical breakthroughs that enabled cinema verité and the dawning of the video age with the introduction of portable video equipment in 1967 inspired many to again see documentary as a tool within political movements.

Seeing themselves as a cultural vanguard for change, activist filmmakers—often students or ex-students in a university community—formed collectives, or projects where work and benefits were shared equally. In the United States, newsreel collectives dedicated to raising awareness of social injustice among working people emerged in New York, San Francisco, and Chicago. In France, in the period that culminated in the 1968 general strike, Jean-Luc Godard and others formed the significantly named but short-lived Dziga Vertov group, which experimented with avant-garde film approaches. Chris Marker and others formed the more militant Iskra, named after Lenin's underground newspaper and focused more on working issues. In British collectives such as the London Film-Makers Co-op and the London Women's Film Co-op, members debated what styles were effective and which audiences to target.

Links were often international. In South Africa and worldwide, antiapartheid activists used *End of the Dialogue (Phela-Ndaba*, 1971) to rally international support. The film, which grimly exposed the harsh contrasts between wealthy white daily life and that of blacks in South Africa, was made by exiles in London. In India, the activist filmmaker Anand Patwardhan worked with demonstrators to document their struggle against government corruption. He smuggled out the footage and took a job in Canada; there, with resisters to India's emergency government, he made *Waves of Revolution* (1975). Internationally shown (but banned in India), it was used by political organizations to rally opposition to the emergency.

Throughout Latin America, filmmakers worked in groups inspired by the Cuban revolution's resistance to U.S. hegemony, and thus evolved a notion of "third cinema," a term that came to describe activist cinema around the world. Filmmakers in the developing world seized upon this idea, as did filmmakers in all parts of the globe who felt marginalized or saw themselves as representing the oppressed.

"Third cinema" derived from the concept of "Third World," which refers to nations and cultural movements that demanded autonomy from the superpower struggle of the Cold War. It promised a view of political change that was not tied to the now-discredited Soviet Communist Party. Intellectuals and artists worldwide saw culture as an arm of this movement. Latin American independent and dissident cinema—*nuevo cine* and in Brazil *cinema novo*—led the way and, as Michael Chanan stated, documentary was an important feature of it.

Cuba, where the film industry was nationalized by 1960, was a center of production and support for independent filmmakers under attack in their own countries. (Joris Ivens worked with some of Cuba's leading filmmakers in the 1960s.) Cuban photographer and filmmaker Santiago Alvarez started Cuba's own version of Kino Eye newsreels and made many documentaries himself. The films show not only passionate outrage at injustice but also lyrical support for the revolution. One of Alvarez's first documentary efforts was *Now* (1965), interesting for its reuse of found images. Here, Alvarez composed a denunciation of racism in the United States with a collage from photos in magazines and newspapers of racial conflict. The soundtrack features Lena Horne singing a freedom song.

In Argentina, Fernando Birri established a socially engaged film school whose first film, *Tire Dié* (*Throw Me a Dime*, 1960) showed how young children raised money to feed their families by begging for coins from passengers on passing trains. Largely uncommented, borrowing in part from the neorealist style Birri had studied in Italy, the film follows the youngsters in tracking shots as they run beside the train: it denounces by revealing.

As Argentine politics polarized, filmmakers mentored or inspired by Birri participated in organized resistance or armed struggle, often were persecuted and many even "disappeared."

Among the most influential filmmakers of the movement were Argentine filmmaker Fernando Solanas and Argentine sociologist Octavio Getino, who together produced a brash and tremendously influential manifesto calling for a "third cinema." (Hollywood and "art," or auteur cinema, were the first two.) They asserted that cinema should not merely be a "hammer," as Grierson had described it, but in itself be an act of "decolonization." Their goal was to "dissolve aesthetics into the life of the society," making intellectuals just as relevant to revolution as the masses. In theory, such films would be made by revolutionary teamwork and be shown in "liberated space." Spectators would disappear, and collectively produced art would incite viewers to act. Such cinema would wage war against the most potent enemy—the one inside all of us, resisting the creation of a revolutionary "new man" such as the Cubans were making.

Solanas and Getino tried out their theory in *Hour of the Furnaces* (*La Hora de los hornos*, 1968), within the Colectivo Cine Liberación. In three parts totaling more than four hours, the film alternately assaults, engages, explains, and meditates. It is an argument, delivered by an enraged professor shaking his students by the lapels. The first section deals with neocolonialism in Argentina; the second with the rise of the Argentine corporatist president—deeply beloved by the working class—Juan Perón, and with opposition to the coup that displaced him in 1955; the third considers roads to a revolutionary future. Devices are used to trouble and shock: intertitles with words that multiply, blank screens, and a full five-minute focus on the dead face of Che Guevara, to whom the film is dedicated.

The film was shown clandestinely in Argentina and in other Latin American countries, and widely throughout the world at film festivals and in theaters. In the United States, *The Hour of the Furnaces* was popular with radical political groups; in Chicago, for instance, the Puerto Rican turf-gang-turned-Maoist-group Young Lords showed it. Solanas, Getino, and many others soon fled into exile.

Other noteworthy films of "third cinema" were completed in exile, such as Chilean filmmaker Patricio Guzmán's three-part epic *The Battle of Chile* (*La Batalla de Chile*, 1975–79). Guzmán was another of those Joris Ivens trained. He had filmed Ivens's 1969 *Valparaiso, Mi Amor*, which poignantly contrasts the rich and poor aspects of the Chilean port city. (Chris Marker wrote the narration for this city symphony.)

Battle is composed of precious verité footage rescued from a three-year film project chronicling the Salvador Allende presidency. The project dissolved when a military coup overthrew Allende; Guzmán smuggled out the footage and fled to Europe. The project now became one to mobilize resistance to the military government internationally. It was completed in France, with the help of leftist film clubs, and in Cuba's nationalized film organization ICAIC, and it was circulated throughout the world, except in Chile. *Battle* indicts some parts of the Chilean military, the Chilean middle class, and the U.S. government for the overthrow of a legitimate, elected government. Crisply suspenseful editing and minimalist narration chart the path toward tragedy.

Filmmakers' interest in "third cinema," cinema verité, and the political power of grassroots testimony converged in projects launched across the world. In Japan, a filmmaking group led by Shinsuke Ogawa documented the protests of peasants resisting the building of the Narita airport. One of the films, *Peasants of the Second Fortress* (1971), showed in rented municipal halls throughout Japan, in coordination with various leftist groups and had a broad international distribution. Shinsuke Ogawa ended up spending his life in such work; after years living with the Narita villagers, he moved to the small village of Magino and made several films documenting daily life there. In another Japanese film, residents of a small fishing village, poisoned by mercury caused by factory discharge, worked with filmmaker Noriaki Tsuchimoto to document their struggle for justice. *Minamata* (1971) raised international awareness of mercury poisoning and shamed the Japanese government into acknowledging the problem. Tsuchimoto continued to use film to raise international awareness and to work with Minamata villagers to keep up pressure to address their mercury-related problems. In Taiwan, the government of the 1970s frowned on acknowledging the oppression of native Taiwanese. A group of artists in the later 1970s produced a TV documentary series, *Fragrant Jewel Island*, celebrating the beauty of native culture. It led not only to a sequel series but to a shared vocabulary of social criticism.

In repressive Soviet-dominated regimes, where freedom of speech was nonexistent and opposition organizations quashed, documentarians inserted criticism directly or indirectly into their works, thus sneaking past censors. The so-called "black" or dissident documentary flourished in Soviet Eastern Europe. Polish filmmakers such as Edward Skorzewski and Krzysztof Kieslowski made acutely observed documentaries designed to provide a disturbing mirror to their audiences.

Advocacy films of the 1960s and 1970s, like those of other eras, combined idealism and pragmatism. They used all of the approaches that the early documentarians had pioneered. Realist and neorealist strategies in the Flaherty tradition, such as those employed in *Tire Dié*, exposed viewers to new realities. Griersonian social mandates pervaded the projects, but now in service of overthrowing rather than preserving the state. Vertov's exuberant formal challenges underlay experiments by Godard, and Cuban documentaries showed influence of Soviet filmmakers. Advocates fiercely debated their formal choices. They also seized upon innovations that could make their work more vivid. Cinema verité equipment and techniques were quickly incorporated. Pragmatism, however, ruled; for instance, if narration was needed in a cinema verité documentary to make the point, then narration was used.

Legacies

The example of "committed," "third," or radical filmmaking has traveled well and still resurfaces in times of crisis and opportunity. In South Korea in the 1970s, young people learned of radical trends at French and German cultural centers, and with the 1980 "Seoul Spring"—a political thaw—produced "people's films" on workers' and rural issues, building a base for independent film organizations. The Seoul Visual Collective's vision was "to secure social rights for the masses." In China after 1989, the "new documentary" movement featuring verité rather than bombast implicitly challenged dogma and served to encourage dissent. Wu Wenguang's *Bumming in Beijing* (1991), about fringe artists in the big city, was a landmark film for urban activists. In early twenty-first century Argentina, after the national financial collapse, film collectives surfaced as agents of political mobilization, making films with political and labor groups.

Many institutions have emerged from activist filmmaking. Distributors such as the Canadian DEC; the American distributors Women Make Movies (a feminist distributor), Third World Newsreel (focusing on socially critical work by people of color), California Newsreel (featuring African American, African, race, and labor issues), New Day (a collective fostering self-distribution); the French Iskra, and others are all legatees of 1960s committed filmmaking. Organizations begun to showcase grassroots and regional voices, such as the U.S. organizations DCTV and Appalshop, have endured and trained new generations of filmmakers. Cable access centers, a U.S. phenomenon of cable channels dedicated to airing films made by and for the local public, developed out of media activism of the era. American filmmaker

George Stoney, who had learned much from his work in 1968–70 with the Canadian Challenge for Change program, was the leader of the movement.

Many other filmmakers eventually took their idealism and filmmaking skills into more traditional arenas, particularly those in public and public service television and higher education. Many American documentarians began their careers in political activism and extended their reach to much broader audiences. For instance, Barbara Kopple, who studied in the late 1960s with the cinema verité pioneers Maysles brothers, made *Harlan County, U.S.A.* (1973) in coordination with striking Kentucky coal miners. The film was important to workers and labor unions, and it won an Academy Award that year. Kopple continued to work with social justice organizations and nonprofits, at the same time directing television dramas and producing commercial documentaries such as *Wild Man Blues* (1997)—a musical tour of film director and jazz musician Woody Allen.

Organizations that took root in this period also developed to produce very different work. Three graduates of the University of Chicago, who were inspired by the work of John Dewey and the capacities of the newly mobile camera, founded the Chicago-based Kartemquin Films. Their first film, *Home for Life* (1966), was a cinema verité view of the indignities of nursing-home life. The film failed to change any health care policies. Looking for more action-oriented projects, and now a political collective, Kartemquin made *The Chicago Maternity Center Story* (1976) to protest the closing of the last public midwifery program in Chicago and as part of a campaign against corporatized health care. After the dissolution of the collective, Kartemquin continued to make films, now oriented at general audiences. Steve James's *Hoop Dreams* (1994) became an international hit after winning an award at the Sundance Film Festival. A seven-hour epic television series, *The New Americans* (2002), co-executive-produced by Kartemquin cofounder Gordon Quinn and Steven James, tracked immigrants to the United States

9. Kartemquin Films' social-change goals were expressed differently at different times; above, Naima in Jerusalem talks to her fiancé in the United States, in *The New Americans* (2004). Produced by Kartemquin Films.

from their native countries. The same concern with giving voice to the subjects, inviting viewers respectfully into the experiences of those subjects, and provoking questions about the status quo that had driven Kartemquin's original work continued in evidence.

When seen later, advocacy films become partisan testimony to history, such as *The Spanish Earth* and *Hour of the Furnaces*. Indeed, *Battle of Chile* has had a new life in Chile after the return of democracy; it now is being used to teach history to Chileans whose Pinochet-era books virtually erased the Allende years.

In the twenty-first century, with ever more sophisticated production equipment, advocacy organizations are both commissioning and producing documentaries as a part of their strategic communications plans. Brave New Films's *Iraq for Sale* (2006), about corporate greed in the Iraq war, and the conservative Citizens United's *Border War* (2006), about immigration into the United States, are both designed as weapons in a war of ideas. When the U.S. Congress considered opening up the Arctic National Wildlife Refuge for oil drilling, the Sierra Club and other environmentally concerned nonprofits produced *Oil on Ice* (2004). This film, narrated by Peter Coyote, examines the battle over oil development within the Arctic National Wildlife Refuge and its impact on both the environment and indigenous communities. It was shown in theaters, on public TV, and in many grassroots settings; the DVD also featured a short film and organizing toolkit. Organizers credited it with mobilizing nationwide awareness and resistance, which, in the end, contributed to the defeat of legislation to initiate oil drilling.

Whatever the perspective, advocacy organizations and nonprofits are beneficiaries of the implicit pledge of documentary to be telling an important story about real life in good faith. Advocacy films maintain that pledge not only through the credibility of their organizations but through the devices they use that signal their reliability. These include (but certainly do not exhaust) the use of authoritative narrators (such as the celebrity Peter Coyote), the realistic portrayal of daily life (*The Spanish Earth*), bold contrast (such as was used in *Borinage*), the use of cinema verité (*Battle of Chile*), statistics in service of argument (*Hour of the Furnaces*), and expert interviews (*Iraq for Sale, Border Wars*). If dueling documentaries become a standard feature of political warfare, however, they could erode the credibility that the form has accrued from its association with embattled causes and issues slighted by a sensationalistic and celebrity-happy mass media.

Historical

"History is not self-executing," wrote historian Arthur Schlesinger Jr. "You do not put a coin in the slot and have history come out." All history is written for people in the present, searching out for them what historians call a "useable past"—a story that is used in the construction of our understanding of ourselves. History is also written on top of an earlier narrative—sometimes disagreeing, sometimes reinforcing, sometimes asserting a presence where previously there was only an absence.

Documentarians who tell history with film encounter all the challenges facing their filmmaking peers. They face historians' problems with getting data. Often they represent events for which there is no film, and as often they represent events using material never intended as a historical record. They turn to photographs, paintings, representative objects, images of key documents, reenactments, and, famously, on-camera experts to substitute for images. They record music that evokes an era, they find singers to sing songs of the time, they build in sound effects to enhance a viewer's sense that what is shown is a genuine moment from the past. They struggle with the question of how much reenactment is appropriate and how it should be achieved.

They also face problems of expertise. Documentary filmmakers typically reach many more people with their work than academic historians do, but filmmakers rarely have the training of historians. Indeed, filmmakers often avoid consulting a range of experts. Too often for filmmakers' liking, historians may be sticklers for precise historical sequences, discussion of multiple interpretations, and the need to insert minor characters or precise accuracies, all of which frustrate the clarity of filmed storytelling for broad audiences. Public service television often requires professional advisory boards, but commercial television productions rarely make such requirements.

Finally, unlike print historians who can digress, comment, and footnote, documentarians work in a form where images and sounds create an imitation of reality that is itself an implicit assertion of truth. This makes it harder for them to introduce alternative interpretations of events or even the notion that we do in fact interpret events.

Documentary filmmakers have often chosen to ignore the implications of their choices: they may accept an uncritical notion that they are merely reporting the facts of the past, or they may adopt uncritically a partisan view of the past. Their works, however, are often the first door through which people walk to understand the past.

Stories

The fact that all historical documentaries are stories of a "useable past" can be illustrated with several examples.

When the Russian revolution was young, filmmaker Esfir Shub created a critical history of czarist rule in *The Fall of the Romanov Dynasty* (1927)—entirely using footage from the czarist archives, including the czar's home movies. Shub had made what would come to be called a "compilation film." Indeed, the czar's family would have been shocked to see their records of luxurious living juxtaposed to images of poverty and misery. Shub had transformed the meaning of the material by her choice of assembly and juxtapositions, from loving records of a privileged family to a damning condemnation of an overthrown government.

Cold War histories from opposite sides, using government archives that had burgeoned with governments' substantial investment in propaganda during World War II, also demonstrate the "usability" of history. Stories were told appropriate to the audience—Communist or capitalist—and to the time. In the new East Germany, the German couple Andrew Thorndike (a German American born and raised in Germany) and Annelie Thorndike produced many works based largely on archival footage, including a celebratory and panoramic view of Russian history, *The Russian Miracle* (1963). In the United States, Henry "Pete" Salomon, a retired U.S. Navy public relations man at NBC networks, worked with the navy to use its footage for *Victory at Sea*, a long-running, twenty-six-part series celebrating the navy's role in the Pacific in World War II. Scored by Richard Rodgers to orchestrate emotional response to the silent film, the aptly titled *Victory at Sea* portrayed the United States and its allies as unselfishly battling for freedom, unstintingly heroic, and of course, ultimately victorious. Both the East German and the American makers worked hard to tell meaningful, emotionally rich stories honestly. Their work also fit neatly within the ideological missions of their governments and era. In later years, when the ideological assumptions of the moment had shifted and thus made visible earlier ones, they were seen as tendentious.

Ken Burns's series *The Civil War* (1990) was also a highly crafted narrative, not merely a recounting of facts. One of the most popular programs on U.S. public television, the series tells us that the Civil War created, for the first time, a unitary American national identity. It employs meditative, moving-camera views of still photographs and the testimony of experts to make this argument. The facticity of the photographs, among other things, gives the viewers the sense that they are merely watching a recital of the facts.

Some southerners might contest the validity of *The Civil War*'s central theme, but the theme reflected, as Gary Edgerton wrote in *Ken Burns's America*, the center of consensus history of its time, a "liberal pluralist perspective" focused on preservation of the Union. Burns faced criticism by historians who espoused other interpretations, and by those who said that the series' real sin was obscuring the fact that it was interpreting rather than reciting history. Burns simply sidestepped this criticism by calling himself not a historian but an "emotional archeologist." He said he had searched in the historical record for the "kind of emotion and sympathy that reminds us, for example, of why we agree against all odds as a people to cohere." In other words, he chose characters and incidents that helped him tell the story he chose to tell about the past.

Commercial considerations shape documentarians' decisions about both subject matter and story line. Television documentaries, designed to entertain, have often featured the lighter side of life, including the entertainment industry itself. Fluffy items such as David Wolper's *Hollywood: The Golden Years* (1961) and the French series *The Mad Twenties* were exemplary productions of the network television era. In the multichannel era of television, historical documentaries have filled many hours cheaply, without any claim to providing comprehensive or balanced perspectives, or covering the most significant aspects of a historical era. Their strung-together sequences of public domain material from governments, along with low-cost archival material (often linked with portentous narration), led to the trade term "clip-job."

Limited access to material also constrains the choices of historical documentarians. As copyright terms have been extended for generations into the future, historical documentaries using extensive archival footage not in the public domain have become more and more expensive. Authoritatively researched historical documentaries have always been some of the more expensive of the documentary categories, but copyright clearance costs skyrocketed at the end of the twentieth century as archives merged and large media corporations developed more zealous control of their resources under the threat of digital reproduction. Peter Jaszi and I showed, in our study *Untold Stories,* that some documentarians feared even to undertake ambitious projects. Documentarians in the United States addressed this problem with the *Documentary Filmmakers' Statement of Best Practices in Fair Use,* a guide that dramatically increased filmmakers' abilities use their rights to quote limited amounts of copyrighted material for free and thus expand the range of what they can make.

Biographies

Biographical documentaries—a particular kind of history—boldly reveal the same choice making that reveals all historical work to be an interpretation. Biography is an immensely popular kind of documentary; it features a close focus on a particular person, promising viewers that they will learn about someone who is recognized as important (a politician, a celebrity, an artist, a sports champion), unsuspectingly important (an unknown inventor, an unsung social worker, an untutored artist), or a witness to history (a Holocaust survivor, Hitler's secretary). These stories are character-driven by definition, but the filmmaker must interpret that character for the viewer.

Entire biographical series have showcased on television; PBS's *American Masters* series and A&E's Biography Channel are two examples. They have clearly recognizable styles, and could not be more different. American Masters provides a narrative of an American life within a particular social moment; individual narratives are given a social location with surrounding information on events and trends that shape and are triggered by individual actions and choices. The narrative builds around not only the events of the person's life but the significance of those events within a wider frame. For example, Diane von Furstenberg and Daniel Wolf's *Andy Warhol* recognizes the American artist who was famous for impudent art stunts and parties as a serious artist with a critical passion for American culture. Respectful but not reverential, the film makes the claim that the viewer will now be able to understand the significance and legacy of Andy Warhol.

A&E's biographies, on the other hand, are tightly structured personality profiles, in two varieties: good (often entertainment celebrities) and bad (often criminals). Scholar Mikita Brottman notes that stories are sanitized to represent celebrities as likeable, upstanding citizens, and contradictory evidence is suppressed. For instance, in a biography of Dean Martin that was part of a series on the "Rat Pack" of celebrities around Frank Sinatra, Martin is represented as a dedicated family man, in spite of a wealth of evidence on his womanizing and partying.

However different, each of these series uses filmic techniques intended to bring closure to the viewer's understanding of the character featured. Authorities are quoted reinforcing the story line; selected historical footage emphasizes the point; the end of the film brings together the themes so that viewers will know the significance, the importance, and the meaning for them of this person's life. Some biographies, by contrast, use film techniques to call attention to the constructed nature of the biography, and call into question the viewer's comfortable assumptions. For instance, Kirby Dick and Amy Ziering Kofman's *Derrida* (2002) is a challenge to the established form of biographical documentary; it cleverly enacts the difference between experience and documenting, and reveals the power of the storyteller to assert reality—in part by showing how difficult it is to construct a story. Jacques Derrida, whose life work involved "deconstructing" our assumptions about knowledge, repeatedly refuses to cooperate with the filmmakers, revealing instead their presence. These acts in themselves are also revealing of the character and perspective of the philosopher. The film challenges the viewer to ask the questions Derrida asked about reality and expression. The work of Errol Morris demonstrates another approach to undermining simple associations between biographical truth and documentary. For instance, in his *Fog of War* (2003), Morris permits Robert McNamara, secretary of defense under presidents Kennedy and Johnson, to describe his own life and controversial political and personal decisions at length, and without comment. The complexities and contradictions of McNamara's life are held up for viewers who must wrestle with their own judgments of McNamara.

Revisionism

One of the most interesting ways to see the power of storytelling is in revisionist history films. These are films that challenge the dominant version of the historical record. Documentaries that questioned received wisdom on World War II have greatly affected public knowledge of that history and, in the process, have also produced new primary-source documents for historians. In some cases, they are unique records of first-person accounts of history.

The British series *The World at War* (1973), produced by Jeremy Isaacs for the commercial network Thames TV (during an era when British commercial networks were required to do substantial public service), marked a historic shift in interpretation of World War II. The twenty-six-hour series combining historical footage with eyewitness interviews is still beloved in Britain and has shown all over the world, including on the History Channel. It was revisionist in several ways. *The World at War* took a global view of the war, rather than a national or regional one, and it depended on eyewitnesses. A cadre of dedicated historical researchers—some of them academic historians—found compelling interviewees who could reach Isaacs's goal of showing how war "actually affected ordinary people." Its core message was that war is hell, not that victory was ours. Shocking images of brutal atrocity and death helped to make that message vivid. It had a powerful resonance at a time when the fear of superpower-triggered nuclear war and the reality of superpower-triggered proxy wars were both very much a part of the zeitgeist.

Around the same time, French documentarian Marcel Ophuls reframed international understanding of France's experience of World War II. Ophuls's method was that of investigative reporting, which he applied in *The Sorrow and the Pity* (1969) to the question of collaboration with Nazi domination. He found previously undiscussed depths of unquestioning cooperation with the fascists. The controversial four-and-a-half-hour film was composed largely of interviews in the small town of Clermont-Ferrand, and it revealed that the heroic image of the French Resistance was a myth in France's middle class; it was the working poor who led Resistance efforts. (The filmmaker was later criticized for selecting a town where the Communist Party was unusually poorly represented, since the CP had been a key organizer of Resistance efforts.) Although it was co-produced by French state TV along with West German and Swiss government television and shown in Germany and Switzerland, the French prime minister ordered it banned on French television. After a triumphant U.S. tour, it was shown in French theaters and on the British BBC.

Following in this style of implacable reexamining of World War II history, Claude Lanzmann, a French Jew, produced a nearly ten-hour series, *Shoah* (1985). Depending entirely on interviews with survivors and surviving agents of the Holocaust—usually the technicians and functionaries—Lanzmann methodically pursued the question not of *how* it could have happened, but exactly how it *did* happen (or at least how people remembered it). *Shoah* provided an unprecedentedly specific public record of the mechanisms of mass murder. With its procedural approach, it shocked and moved audiences, and spurred debate on the ethics of interviewing. Were hidden cameras justifiable for recalcitrant subjects? Was restaging an interview appropriate? How much context should be given a viewer?

World War II revisionism not only offered a different perspective with new information but also introduced new elements to the story. In Japan, Kazuo Hara's *The Emperor's Naked Army Marches On* (1988), in cinema verité fashion follows a maniacally obsessed veteran trying to expose cannibalism among troops abandoned in New Guinea after the war and, subtextually, holding the emperor accountable for war crimes that had simply been denied. The veteran's story, grisly and unique, also stands for the denial of war crimes in general. In the United States, feminist filmmaker Connie Field, in making *The Life and Times of Rosie the Riveter* (1980), told a hidden history of women whose wartime jobs changed their lives; it also chronicled the coordinated governmental effort to get these women to give up their jobs and return to the home after the war. Field brought women and workers back into a history that had been dominated by male soldiers and politicians.

One of the most striking examples of bringing new elements into the historical record is Henry Hampton's *Eyes on the Prize* (1987, 1990) series. This breakthrough series on American public television traces the civil rights movement as one that upheld the best values in American culture, often against the racist status quo of the time and not without deep internal conflicts. Teams of paired African American and white producers, working with academic historians as advisors, crafted their stories using rare archival footage drawn from small and large archives, personal collections, and the vaults of local television stations. The series brought to national viewers images and incidents that had been seen by a local television news audience perhaps only once in the past. It created nationwide public awareness of the profound impact of the civil rights movement on American history. The series became a staple in American schools and served as a model for later historically revisionist series such as the four-hour series

Chicano! (1996) and *A Question of Equality* (1996), this latter a history of the gay and lesbian rights movements.

Revisionist documentaries themselves may, of course, leave out crucial information, whether purposefully or not. For example, in American independent documentaries made in the 1970s and 1980s recalling political movements of the 1930s—union organizing (*Union Maids*, 1976), strikes (*With Babies and Banners*, 1978), the Spanish Civil War (*The Good Fight*, 1984)—baby boom-era documentarians often did not reveal the extent of the Communist Party's role in the events or they took at face value the self-reporting of CP members. Depending on oral histories to salvage suppressed elements of the past, and seeing themselves as legatees of political activists they admired, these filmmakers could have easily become prisoners of the limitations of oral history as a sole source of information.

Memory and history

With the growth of home film and video archives and ever-simpler video cameras, the memoir or personal film has made important contributions to historical documentary. In such works, the private and personal are exposed and sometimes contrasted with the official or public record. Individual memory is juxtaposed with and often challenges public history. New stories surface, and individual experience enriches public understanding of the past.

Filmmakers use a variety of techniques to represent memory. One common trope, according to filmmaker David MacDougall, is putting "signs of absence"—images of loss, of objects abandoned, of a photo to be explained—at the center of the film and of the problem to be solved with memory. For instance, the makers of *Into the Arms of Strangers* (2004), about the *Kindertransporte* that whisked Jewish children out of Nazi Germany, sought out and used as symbols the actual objects children had brought with them, rather than merely displaying a similar object. Many times, personal filmmakers also use an ironic or reflexive approach to familiar objects or images, forcing a reanalysis of them: collages, blank images, text that startles or asks questions, and repetition—all of which forces viewers to reflect upon or reinterpret the meaning of a sound or image.

In some cases, filmmakers have drawn from avant-garde and experimental filmmaking from earlier eras. The work of American avant-garde filmmaker Yvonne Rainer offers many good examples. Gay African American filmmaker Marlon Riggs structured *Tongues Untied* (1989) as a visual poem that had the narrative arc of a journey toward owning his identity. Ross McElwee's life's work (*Sherman's March*, 1986; *Six O'Clock News*, 1996; *Bright Leaves*, 2003), which tracks the evolution of the filmmaker's (or his persona's) sense of self, draws from McElwee's own training among experimental filmmakers using the body and their own lives as subject matter.

Personal films contributed to the development of cultural identity movements worldwide in the 1980s and 1990s. Political changes and economic globalization created vast new diasporic movements of South Asians, Southeast Asians, "overseas Chinese," and Africans. Self-consciously diasporic cultures began to emerge and find self-expression in film, with support from institutions encouraging that self-expression. In Britain protests by independent filmmakers, demands of ethnic minorities in the wake of riots, and the launching of the new private (but funded with public revenues) Channel 4 TV coalesced into the formation of special workshops to cultivate filmmaking by minorities.

Among the successful results were the so-called black film workshops, including Sankofa, one of whose celebrated filmmakers was Isaac Julien, and Black Audio Collective. These workshops generated enormous and productive political debates about the self-representation of various minorities and the role of women. One prominent result was John Akomfrah's *Handsworth Songs*

(1986). Unapologetically experimental, it poetically reworked images of riots, slums, newsreels, and colonial historical footage into a personal essay on history and identity. Another heralded work was *Body Beautiful* (1990) by Ngozi Onwurah, the daughter of a Nigerian father and a British mother. The film combines fiction and documentary, using an actress to represent the filmmaker and with the mother playing herself. It contrasts the mother's and daughter's body images and their personal histories, as conditioned by the ordinary racial, gender, and age discrimination of British society.

The postcolonial and post–Cold War era also generated much work that combined an autobiographical impulse with a historical reexamination. Filmmakers turned to the personal essay form to challenge official amnesia in Africa. David Achkar's father, a prominent Guinean official, had fallen from favor and died in prison. Achkar's *Allah, Tantou* (1991) mixes reenactment, family letters, home movies, and newsreel images to challenge the public version of his father's disappearance. The film, as much meditation as memoir, provided a counter to the mythology surrounding revolutionary leader Sekou Touré and generated controversy in Guinea and worldwide. Haitian Raoul Peck, whose family had served Patrice Lumumba's government in Congo, made *Lumumba: Death of a Prophet* (1992). The documentary—Peck later made a fiction film of the same name—weaves together Peck's family's home movies, his own video diary of his fruitless search for archival images of Lumumba that had been suppressed by Lumumba's killer and successor Mobutu, interviews, and news footage. Cameroonian Jean-Marie Teno made a sharply voiced series of personal films, linking colonial history with present brutalities, including *Afrique, Je Te Plumerai* (Africa, I Will Fleece You, 1992).

The end of Latin American dictatorships also brought forward the theme of memory and history. Brazilian Eduardo Coutinho in

10 and 11. Patricio Guzmán's epic *The Battle of Chile* (1976), top, about the downfall of the Allende government, was not shown in Chile until his return 30 years later—a visit recorded in *Chile, Obstinate Memory* (1997), bottom. Directed by Patricio Guzmán.

Cabra Marcado para Morrer (Twenty Years Later, a.k.a. A Man Listed to Die, 1984) returned to a site where, twenty years earlier, his film crew had hastily buried film cans from a *cinema novo* project about the murder of a peasant land reform leader. The project had been halted abruptly by a military coup. Coutinho then tracked down the peasant's widow and eight children. The result was the story of a generation of loss told through the experiences of one shattered family. Chilean director Patricio Guzmán in 1997 made *Chile, Obstinate Memory*, a memoir of his journey home to show *The Battle of Chile*—banned until then—for the first time to his own people.

Personal films have also been a vehicle for reviving public memory of the unthinkable or unbearable. Holocaust memoirs and memory films proliferated in the 1990s: Mira Binford's *Diamonds in the Snow* (1994), Ilan Ziv's *Tango of Slaves* (1994), Amir Bar-Lev's *Fighter* (2001), Oren Rudavsky and Menachem Daum's *Hiding and Seeking* (2004), among many others. Descendants of Holocaust survivors, and sometimes survivors themselves, sought answers, closure, or resolution by returning to the sites, encounters with other survivors, or even confrontation with those from the past. Also exploring the power of private memory to inform the public's knowledge of the past is the work of Hungarian Peter Forgács, who reworks amateur and family footage to create meditations on forgotten and suppressed eastern European history of the 1930s.

Finally, personal-voice and home movies have been interwoven into reexaminations of popular culture. Stacy Peralta's *Dogtown and Z-Boys* (2001), an engaging and lively history of skateboarding culture, tracks its evolution from the gritty side streets of Santa Monica to a billion-dollar business, some of whose celebrities (such as Peralta himself) came from those streets. It interweaves home movies with reminiscence and contrasts both with verité material from the fast-paced and commercialized world of competitive skateboarding. Danish filmmaker Anders Høgsbro Østergaard's *Tintin and I* creates a sensitive psychological biography of the

Belgian writer and artist Hergé, matching intimate audio interviews from the 1970s with animation drawn from contemporary video footage of Hergé and animating his comic-book illustrations as well. Understanding Hergé's journey from Catholic ultraconservative to nearly New Ager through the Cold War period also makes for a reanalysis of his popular comic books.

The growth of personal documentary has provoked scholars to explore the relationship of memory to truth. Linda Williams argues that such films challenge viewers to recognize that truths exist in a context, in relationship to lies, and are selected from other truths. Going beyond reflexivity (that is, calling attention to the fact that the film is a film), such films posit that there are important truths to be revealed and that they can be revealed in spite of—or even by calling attention to—the partiality of our understanding. Thus, such films offer another approach to the problem of how documentaries can be truthful. Bill Nichols states that personal documentaries often "perform" the filmmaker's state of mind and associations, documenting an intimate kind of reality. Michael Renov writes that the often-confessional tone of personal documentaries brings viewers actively into the construction of the film's meaning, thus heightening empathy.

Usable for whom and for what?

Documentarians sometimes chafe at the notion that they must become historians in order to make a historical film. And yet a filmmaker's responsibility to users is a large one. Not only is each documentary taken by viewers and later filmmakers as an accurate representation of the history it shows but also historical knowledge shapes users' understanding of who they are in the present. Jon Else, in making *Cadillac Desert* (1997) about water politics in the United States, said that although many dams looked alike, he insisted on absolute accuracy because he knew that later filmmakers would quote his work rather than going back to the sources he originally used. Every historical film occurs within an ideological frame that deserves to be understood at the very least before being presented to viewers.

If all history is useable history, then what is relevant about a particular story, and to whom is it, and why? These are good questions to ask for makers and viewers alike.

Ethnographic

Ethnographic film is a term with many connotations. Festival programmers, such as those at the standard-setting Margaret Mead Film Festival held each year in New York at the American Museum of Natural History, usually define ethnographic film as one about other cultures, exotic peoples, or customs. Television programmers commission under that rubric documentaries that entertain, whether charmingly or shockingly, with exotic cultural material. Independent filmmakers such as Les Blank, who has explored musical and food subcultures worldwide with empathy and respect, are happy to show their work under that banner. Anthropologists would like to see the term used more scientifically. Anthropologist Jay Ruby argues that only if a film is produced by a trained ethnographer, using ethnographic field methods, and with the intention of making a peer-reviewed ethnography should it be called an ethnographic film.

Linking these various interpretations is the notion of otherness—that ethnographic film is a look from outside a culture, giving you a glimpse inside it. Such a claim raises the stakes on the usual ethical questions of documentary. The relationship between filmmaker and subject is particularly fraught in ethnographic cinema because the subjects are more often than not members of cultural groups with less power in society and media than the filmmaker. Anthropologists relish the story that anthropologist-filmmaker Sol Worth told about Sam Yazzie. Worth, along with John Adair, conducted the Navajo

Film Project in the 1970s. The project strove to teach Navajo Indians techniques of filmmaking without imposing aesthetic or ideological filters. Elder Sam Yazzie, when the project was described, asked, "Will making movies do the sheep any harm?" When the filmmakers assured him that no harm would come to the sheep, Yazzie asked, "Will making movies do the sheep good?" "Well, no," they replied. "Then why make movies?" Worth wrote, "Sam Yazzie's question keeps haunting us."

Making money

The early answer to the "why make movies" question was straightforward: to make money. The exotic adventure film, with crossovers to anthropological practice (chronicling "primitive" cultures, living with subjects, sharing the crafting of narrative with subjects), was established in this period. Flaherty's *Nanook of the North* inspired later anthropological filmmakers. Merian C. Cooper, who had already co-produced an impressive but financially failed travelogue film, *Grass* (1925), about a nomadic tribe, made the box-office hit *Chang* in 1927 and produced the hugely successful *King Kong* (1933). Drawn from an eighteen-month stay with Lao people in northern Siam, *Chang* constructed a viewer-friendly narrative out of daily life. Villagers fight off threats from a leopard and tiger; after a wild elephant stampede (a staged event), the villagers tame the elephants and use them to reconstruct their peaceful jungle life.

The exotic adventure film led to fantasy-filled jungle movies and to "shockumentaries" such as the 1962 *Mondo Cane* and its sequels. In *Mondo Cane*, shocking scenes such as New Guinea tribesmen clubbing a pig to death cut to silly scenes such as elderly students awkwardly learning the Hawai'ian hula dance, with narration and a soundtrack smoothing over incongruities.

More upscale films offered viewers an experience of other cultures, without claiming ethnographic insight but often benefiting from the association. In *Dead Birds* (1963), about life and death in Western Irian Jaya, artist Robert Gardner used license learned from Flaherty to weave a "true story" out of "actual events." Critics heralded his poetic sensibility and his ability to touch on universal themes, and often called his work ethnographic (something Gardner never did). In *Forest of Bliss* (1985), about death rituals and daily life in and around Benares, Gardner created an idiosyncratic but compelling and sometimes gruesome meditation on death and the meaning of life. It was screened for audiences in the global North, who were largely ignorant about the practices shown in the film; South Asians, Hindus, and anthropologists wrung their hands at the lack of cultural context.

Grappling with conventions

As the broadcast television market burgeoned in the 1960s and 1970s, so did series on exotic cultures such as the British Granada TV's *Disappearing World* (1970–93), and the Japanese Nippon TV *Our Wonderful World* (mid-1960s–1982). Viewers were often encouraged—despite the howls of anthropological consultants and sometimes members of the cultural groups themselves—to believe that they were watching uncontaminated cultural practices that one touch by the modern world could destroy.

Most documentaries on cross-cultural issues today do not make clear claims for their purpose. They are typically shown to audiences in the global North about people in other parts of the world. Some of these entertain with good-looking characters, colorful practices, and narratives driven by crisis, ghoulishness, or disaster. They often claim to rescue for civilized viewers a last glimpse of a passing exotic culture, as *The Story of the Weeping Camel* does. The National Geographic *Taboo* series (2003 on) shows viewers bizarre body-decoration practices around the world on one week, and weird food people eat on the next. Other work strives to take viewers inside someone else's experience unpretentiously. For example, Dutch director Leonard Retel Helmrich's *Shape of the Moon* (2004), follows, in cinema verité style, a widowed Christian woman in Jakarta as her son converts to Islam, giving Western viewers a glimpse of cultural conflicts they may not even have imagined.

Most producers on cross-cultural subjects find themselves bound by the conventions of mass media, which work against reflexivity, experiment, and open interpretation. The work of Australians Robin Anderson and Bob Connelly is interesting as a healthy struggle with the limits of the commercial medium. In their widely broadcast first film, *First Contact* (1983), they brought to Papua New Guinean villagers footage of the first time whites—male prospectors—had encountered them. The prospector's record of their exploration was re-seen through the eyes of the villagers. The film also traces the ever-widening consequences of the encounter, which brought the Papuans unasked-for pregnancies, diseases, machinery, and a tourist economy.

First Contact, which had two sequels, fascinates for its deft juggling of reflexivity within realist conventions. It asks viewers to critically reexamine the early footage and also reassures them of a stable meaning in Anderson and Connelly's own footage—through its editing, its tight narrative focus, and its explicit and implicit explanations of what viewers saw.

Scientific?

Social scientists first imagined ethnographic film as a scientific tool. Early anthropologists, such as Franz Boas (founder of the field), Margaret Mead, and Gregory Bateson made short, purely descriptive films of discrete routines and acts. For decades, the Göttingen Institute for Scientific Films in Germany commissioned five-minute sequences, accompanied by written texts, on specific rituals and production techniques. Substantial archives of such material exist internationally today. However, these archives raise questions that were not always obvious to those recording the images at the time. What do these acts mean to the people doing them? What kind of inquiry does this information serve? Were the people reenacting something or being caught in the act of doing something they always do?

Anthropologists and anthropologically trained filmmakers soon began exploring these questions. As a privileged teenager on safari with his father, the American John Marshall first became familiar with Kalahari nomads. A few years later, he made *The Hunters* (1957) from silent footage he took with the San (known as Bushmen to whites in South Africa at that time). He openly aspired to be the Flaherty of the Kalahari, celebrating the successful struggle of the nomads against nature. A commercial hit and widely seen in classrooms, the film was also criticized for its romanticism. The controversies provoked rethinking, and Marshall recut his footage into a series of educational films with, among others, the young photographer Timothy Asch, who then pursued an anthropology degree. Single-focus, short films accompanied by discussion material became popular in teaching.

Marshall went on to work with pioneers of the cinema verité movement, including Fred Wiseman (for whom he shot *Titicut Follies*), D A Pennebaker, and Flaherty's protégé Richard Leacock. In 1980, with Adrienne Linden, Marshall made a biography of one of his South African subjects and incorporated footage he had taken of her over three decades in which the rights of the San had badly eroded. *N!ai: The Story of a !Kung Woman* (1980), made for American public TV, contrasted sharply with the romantic isolation of his first film and chronicled Marshall's growing awareness of the power of the filmmaker in relation to the subject.

After his work with Marshall, Tim Asch went on to collaborate with anthropologist Napoleon Chagnon, who worked in lowlands Brazil with the Yanomami tribe. There, he and Chagnon produced a large body of work and also explored how to represent their own understanding and experience of Yanomami culture. *The Ax Fight* (1975) was a triumph of their collaboration and a critique of ethnographic film approaches up to that time. In the film, Asch and Chagnon witnessed and filmed two-thirds of an ax fight in a village. Asch provided several versions: a simple presentation of all the footage he had; a version that used slow motion and guiding arrows to show more clearly participants and events; an analysis of kinship relations; and a smoothly edited narrative reminiscent of what students had been used to seeing. Thus, *The Ax Fight* forced viewers to ask themselves how they would interpret what they saw. Although it did not result in many imitators (possibly because the model was not commercially viable), it precipitated an anthropological debate about how best to use film.

Jean Rouch

From the 1960s, disenchantment with claims of scientific objectivity created turmoil in the discipline of anthropology. At the same time, ethnographically inclined filmmakers were fascinated by cinema verité. Riding these two waves was anthropologist and filmmaker Jean Rouch, one of the most creative forces in ethnographic film and one of its most vigorous challengers.

Rouch, an engineer whose work in West Africa prompted him to study anthropology on his return to France, ultimately made more than one hundred films, many of them in collaboration with his subjects. He drew inspiration from both Flaherty and Vertov. He respected Flaherty's affectionate relationship with his subjects and his participatory approach; he admired Vertov for his passion for capturing life as it was, and then seizing the right to edit that reality, forcing the viewer to acknowledge the presence of the filmmaker.

Rouch's first major film caused him to rethink his earlier approach. *Les Maîtres Fous* (1955) took viewers inside a weekend spiritual ritual in which West African migrant workers in Ghana went into trances, playing roles that imitated colonial officials. Rouch's ending narration suggested that this ritual was both an expression of and a temporary release from their colonial existence. The film shocked Europeans and horrified Africans, who were afraid that Europeans would see them as uncivilized. After the end of colonialism, leftist critics excoriated the ending as patronizing.

Although Rouch never repudiated the film, he began to work more collaboratively with his subjects. He also unceasingly experimented with how to explore their subjectivity, often turning to fiction, fantasy, and role-playing. For instance, in *Moi, un Noir* (1957) young Songhay men assumed the roles of characters they created—out of the fabric of their own lives—in a collaboratively made film about a week in the life of a migrant worker. Rouch had begun to articulate an approach that used the camera as a provocation or catalyst to reveal social tension, one he took further in looking at his own "tribe" of Parisians in *Chronicle of a Summer*.

His goal was to challenge unreflective approaches to both science and art in film. On the subject of anthropology, Rouch said he wanted to transform it from "the elder daughter of colonialism, a discipline reserved to people with power interrogating people without it. I want to replace it with a shared anthropology... an anthropological dialogue between people belonging to different cultures, which to me is the discipline of human sciences for the future." About documentary, he said that for him

> there is almost no boundary between documentary film and films of fiction. The cinema, the art of the double, is already the transition from the real world to the imaginary world, and ethnography, the science of the thought systems of others, is a permanent crossing point from one conceptual universe to another; acrobatic gymnastics, where losing one's footing is the least of the risks.

Rouch made films about other people for three reasons. First, of course, he made them for himself, then for general audiences. Third, he made them because "film is the only method I have to show another just how I see him" and if it were participatory.

It became a way of changing the anthropological relationship: "Thanks to feedback, the anthropologist is no longer an entomologist observing his subject as if it were an insect (putting it down) but rather as if it were a stimulant for mutual understanding (hence dignity)." Even today, people concerned with questions of power and meaning in ethnographic film turn back to Jean Rouch.

Made with...

Ethnographic filmmakers have built on Rouch's courageous creativity in finding ways to bridge the power gap between subject and maker, and they also experimented on their own. David and Judith MacDougall, who studied anthropology and did graduate work in film, have produced distinctive and thoughtful work embodying and expostulating a theory of "participatory cinema," a term they prefer to "cinema verité" although their work is classically observational. The MacDougalls' films share an open respect for the cultural habits and choices of the subjects of the film, without asking viewers to like or sympathize with them. In *The Wedding Camels: A Turkana Marriage* (1976) the MacDougalls followed the process by which a wedding was negotiated among a group in Kenya whom they knew well. The film reveals a profoundly different notion of marriage from the contemporary Western one. At the same time, the MacDougalls' choices also express their own convictions: their films on the Turkana are implicit endorsements of the right of pastoralists to live as pastoralists. David MacDougall states that he wants "to reclaim documentary as an arena of engagement with the world, one that actively confronts reality, and that in so doing is transformed into a mode of inquiry in its own right."

Participation by the subjects has also been part of an engaged, anticolonial practice, as *Taking Pictures* (1996), about a generation of ethnographic filmmakers in Australia and New Zealand, documents well. In the 1960s and 1970s, as Australians began to reconsider their relationship to the indigenous population and as New Guinea gained independence in 1975, anthropologists and filmmakers saw themselves as progressives working for and sometimes with native peoples to recover their dignity and self-image. These projects raised many of the questions filmmakers and anthropologists confronted in making them.

Australian anthropologist Jerry Leach, filmmaker Gary Kildea, and a Trobriand Island (part of Papua New Guinea) political association jointly worked to make *Trobriand Cricket* (1979). The film follows the game of cricket the islanders adapted from their ex-colonial masters so thoroughly that it has become an elegant expression of their own culture. They used the game to make a transition from deadly warfare to game-based and symbolic warfare; far from victims in need of salvage ethnography they, like Rouch's subjects, are creative cultural innovators. The film spoke to whites by whites and to Trobriand Islanders, about themselves. Filmmakers can also reverse the camera. Australian Dennis O'Rourke worked with Papuans to make the acerbic *Cannibal Tours* (1987), in which the exotic subjects were the tourists who came to visit Papua and who frequently baffled the natives with their bizarre customs.

Made by...

Concern with participation and sharing in ethnographic filmmaking, along with the rising demands of indigenous groups and new nations, led to the growth of indigenous production. It changed the field of visual anthropology as well; Faye Ginsburg and others began to argue that the field must concern itself with the anthropology of media. One large question within that topic has been the ability of the traditional subjects of ethnographic work to make their own media. Ginsburg, Eric Michaels, George Stoney, and Lorna Roth have all been as much champions of indigenous expression as analysts of it.

Empowering indigenous creators became a movement in the 1970s, fueled by "Fourth World," "First Nations," or indigenous activism and thereby lowered costs of video. In Canada, the National Film Board's Challenge for Change program, intended to strengthen community integration and ability of Canada's underrepresented communities to represent themselves, worked with native activists. Films such as *You Are on Indian Land* (1969), a record of a protest by Mohawk Indians of a treaty violation, and *Cree Hunters of the Mistassini* (1974), a celebration of the hunter-gatherer culture of the northern Cree menaced by a hydroelectric project, were made and used as part of campaigns to reclaim land and land-use rights. Canadian native peoples learned from these interactions as they negotiated for communications systems for the region that in 1999 became autonomous.

In Latin America, Brazilian Indians learned to use video to record traditional culture through the Video in the Villages project.

12. Through the Video in the Villages project, Amazonian Indians made films like *Cheiro de Pequi* (The Smell of the Pequi Fruit) that put ethnographic filmmaking into the first-person. Directed by Takumã Kuikuro and Maricã Kuikuro, with Vincent Carelli, 2006.

They used it to revive traditional practices, to create a record of their negotiations with white people, and eventually to tell myths and stories of their own lives to others. Some of the work, aimed at outsiders, used a deliberately naïve perspective, such as the video letter format of *From the Ikpeng Children to the World* (2004). In other cases, Indians recounted myths or recorded ceremonies with goals such as preserving knowledge and enhancing awareness of their cultural wealth. In still others, such as *Cheiro de Pequi* (The Smell of the Pequi Fruit, 2006), the Indians (in this case the Kuikuro) connect the mythic past with present ceremony and daily life.

In Australia, aboriginal groups produced work describing their struggles, such as *Two Laws* (1981), produced with help from a community group, about the need to recognize aboriginal laws and customs. Aboriginal artists such as Tracey Moffatt created work that not only documented experience but used experimental and fictional approaches to do so. Aboriginal youth have created, in Us Mob, both an ongoing video project and an online website and community. In Finland, Samí director Paul-Anders Simma, in *Legacy of the Tundra* (1995) showed outsiders the culture of reindeer herding under ecological strain.

People in dominant cultures have often worried about the effect of media production on indigenous cultures. Indigenous filmmakers and activists have typically found this concern either baffling or insulting. Typically, the concern depends on a static conception of traditional culture, rather than seeing culture as the flexible social skin that takes on new shapes with new information, such as that seen in *Trobriand Cricket*. Indigenous activists argue that they are also inevitably bombarded with modern media and communications, and should be permitted access to expression as well as consumption. If, at the same time, indigenous people lack the ability to tell and transmit their own stories (since they have little control over much of the mass media that comes to them), mass media can become what

Faye Ginsburg calls a "Faustian contract," where they sell their cultural souls for access to media. As with all other social inequalities, the power imbalance is rarely solved with a technical fix.

For whom and for what?

Is ethnographic film for scientists, its subjects, or television audiences? Can there be overlaps or common goals? This is still a hotly debated question. So far anthropologists have not found funding or intellectual armature for a scientific method. Teachers regularly use work that was designed for a commercial or quasi-commercial television market. Indigenous people often have had clearly defined and practical reasons for their work: creating a record, warning authorities, exchanging cultural information with other cultural groups, educating whites. They rarely reach mass media and broad audiences in the global North, however.

The challenges that documentaries on cultural issues and practices face in crossing cultural boundaries, both with subjects and users, are the challenges that Jean Rouch addressed with unfailing optimism, and that have always been at the heart of anthropology.

Nature

Animals were among the first subjects for filmmakers—cute pets, dead trophies, and exotic creatures. As documentary grew in commercial importance, so did the animal subjects, who cost less than actors. The nature documentary, also called environmental, conservationist, or wildlife, is now a major subgenre, an established part of the broadcast schedule and a dynamic category. Nature documentaries, which at first glance seem to be straightforward and ideologically neutral, expose our assumptions about our relationships with our environment.

Educational entertainment

Early nature films were driven by two seemingly opposing goals: science, and entertainment. Over time, the two impulses merged into the malleable claim of entertaining education.

In the late nineteenth century, scientific experiments with photography—including a French physiologist's invention to record birds in flight—pushed forward the creation of motion pictures. Scientists seized upon cinema as a way to document objectively their observations, but not only did they inevitably edit and design their films (something not always obvious to other scientists), mitigating the pure observational quality, but they also privileged the visual aspect of scientific observation. More general interest documentaries popularized scientific knowledge. An early British series of short documentaries, which ran from 1922 to 1933, called *Secrets of Nature*, presaged later nature series.

At the same time, entertainers looked to film as the next step beyond slide shows of travelogues and hunting expeditions. One of the first documentaries, *Hunting the White Bear* (1903), triggered a wave of chase films. Some safarigoers brought along their personal filmmakers, simply to create trophy records. British photographer Cherry Kearton's record of Theodore Roosevelt's African safari, titled *Roosevelt in Africa* (1910), also featured trophies, but audiences preferred action. Predictably, filmmakers began faking or staging scenes and slaughtering animals to get their footage. (For a critical look at early travelogue films, watch the 1986 compilation film *From the Pole to the Equator*, which links safari films with other imperial adventures.)

Following the success of *Nanook of the North* and *Chang*, Martin and Osa Johnson developed a highly successful commercial business producing nature film, including commercial tie-ins with adventure clothing. Wealthy backers funded a four-year trip to Africa, which resulted in *Simba* (1928). In it, the Johnsons portrayed themselves living a simple, pre-industrial life on "Lake Paradise." They gave names to the animals shown in the film—including the noble lion—and turned Africans themselves into comical wildlife as well. *Simba* was a huge success in theaters and inspired many other, cheaper films.

The thrill of seeing dangerous animals has never truly gone away. Steve Irwin's *The Crocodile Hunter* television series, an international hit until his death in 2006, depended on his risk taking.

In contrast to the violence-filled safari film was the film showing the exquisite balance of nature. Here, man was the dangerous intruder. The work of Swedish filmmaker Arne Sucksdorff, whose lyrical nature documentaries became worldwide hits, exemplified and distilled this style. His best-known feature documentary, *The Great Adventure* (1953), featured a young boy's lyrical view of nature. Sucksdorff's work inspired other bucolic films; perhaps the best known was Georges Rouquier's *Farrebique* (1946), which chronicled the seasons on a French farm.

Disney's nature

The Walt Disney studio synthesized themes of danger, noble savagery, and reverence in the pioneering True-Life Adventure series, launched with the 1948 Academy Award–winning short film *Seal Island*. The Disney films, which originally could not find a distributor and forced Disney to open its own Buena Vista studios, ended up on broadcast television. These films became enormously popular and profitable worldwide. In fact, the series may have saved Disney studios from failure after its expensive animation films bombed at the box office.

In these films, dramatic narrative was driven by a tooth-and-claw Darwinism. The sight of death, however, was discreetly managed for general audiences, and death was always purposeful. For instance, *Seal Island* ignores the fact that seal bulls sometimes

trample pups by accident. The drama of True-Life Adventures—
the first was *The Living Desert* (1953)—was driven by techniques of
fiction cinema. Broad and breathtaking wide-screen panoramas
instill awe; expert pacing ensures suspense; music is portentous or
tittering.

Human beings are absent, but animals play human roles strangely
like a postwar suburban American nuclear family—protective
mothers, concerned fathers, rambunctious children.

True-Life Adventures took place in a time and place comfortably
removed from that of the viewer; any trace of human beings was
carefully expunged. Photographers were told to choose sites where
there was virtually no whiff of civilization. *The Vanishing Prairie*'s
(1954) narration promised to take viewers to a place in "a time
without record or remembrance, when nature alone held dominion
over the prairie realm."

Blue chip and IMAX

True-Life Adventures spurred the creation of long-running
international series such as the British *Nature* films (1982). The
so-called blue chip documentary became a staple of international
documentary production for broadcast. Such documentaries
feature large animals, an absence of humans or human influence,
and a dramatic narrative driven by reproduction and predation
(sex and violence). *Blue Planet*, the BBC/Discovery Channel series
produced in 2001, provides an excellent example. This
breathtaking series, full of technological wizardry and natural
wonder, explores the oceans of the world without much of a hint
that human action is changing conditions for the extraordinary
animals it features.

Large-format IMAX films depend on blue-chip assumptions in
order to draw museum and event audiences to their large-screen
spectacle. Insects (*Bugs! in 3-D*, 2003), large animals (*Dolphins!*,
2000), and a host of shark films all immerse viewers in stories

of natural marvels with little human interference. The rising popularity of documentaries in theaters in the early twenty-first century was also buoyed by blue-chip nature drama. The French Jacques Perrin's *Winged Migration* (2001) offers viewers astonishing close-ups of birds taking off, in flight, and landing to conduct their seasonal migrations. Far from capturing nature, however, the production team actually raised the birds themselves so that the animals would not be afraid of the cumbersome machinery. Luc Jacquet's highly popular international hit *March of the Penguins* (2005), also French, chronicles the seasonal struggle of penguins to reproduce under the conditions of the Antarctic. The film's love story theme strategically ignores basic penguin realities such as the fact that they mate for only one season and skirts discussion of the global warming threatening the birds' existence.

Environmental

At the same time True-Life Adventures was launched, the environmental movement was born in conservation and preservation efforts. The 1950s television series *The Living Earth*, backed by the Conservation Society, deeply penetrated the K-12 educational market. These documentaries stressed the role of human actions on the balance of nature. As environmental consciousness grew, these themes have become more and more common. Nonetheless, substantial artifice goes into even conservationist programming. Most such programs use realism to depict the relationships they show, employing strategic staging, elision editing, and scripting to tell their stories: One animal may actually be made up of shots of several animals; animals' behavior may be provoked, to get exciting footage; most shark films depend on teasing sharks for their action footage. Many nature films minimize or erase the role of the filmmakers; others turn the filmmakers into daring neosafari leaders, as the BBC's *Big Cat* series does.

Some independent filmmakers, however, have challenged viewers to consider their relationship to animals and the natural environment. Australian expatriate Mark Lewis has made a career of raised-eyebrow—and very funny—films about people and animals. *Cane Toads* (1988) looks at the consequences of introducing the cane toad into Australia with savage black humor. This venomous toad had no effect on the beetle it was imported to kill, but it has become a major pest. Lewis's *Rat* (1998) and *Natural History of the Chicken* (2000) chronicle quirky, disgusting, and unusual relationships people have with their all-too-domestic animals. Werner Herzog's *Grizzly Man* (2005) looks at the grim end of Timothy Treadwell, a deranged documentarian who lived in bear country, mistook bears for his friends, and was eaten by one of them. Herzog contrasts Treadwell's misguided sentimentalism with his own nihilism and belief in the inherent cruelty of nature; he matches Treadwell's narcissism with his own and manages to make the bears look more dignified than any of the people in the film.

One of the most successful theatrical documentaries of all time could be considered a nature film: Davis Guggenheim's *An Inconvenient Truth* (2006). Featuring former vice president Al Gore performing a vividly illustrated lecture on global warming, the film puts people in the center of a story about natural calamity. Using dramatic pictures of melting ice, simulations of rising water flooding Manhattan, animation of a drowning polar bear, and astonishing graphs and charts, Gore demonstrates the urgency of the problem. Interwoven are personal reminiscences—his father's farm, the local river, his son's nearly fatal accident, his sister's death. He exposes his failure to convince politicians to act on global warming, saying that they need to hear from their constituents. The combination of scientific data, natural beauty, the jaw-dropping pictures of catastrophe, and personal transformation ready the viewers for the good news at the end: *human action can save our planet.*

These films strikingly contrast with the safari and Disney traditions in nature films because they focus on human action and interaction—not only with animals but with the ecosystems in which we all live. They also help us see what is not in many nature

13. *An Inconvenient Truth*, in which Al Gore made global warming a public concern, created new expectations for environmental filmmaking. Directed by Davis Guggenheim, 2006.

programs and films, and they give us models for new approaches to the stories of our environment.

Significance and ethics

Much critique has focused on the popular films and TV series featuring large animals (BBC's *Big Cat Week* and Discovery Channel's *Shark Week*, for example), asking questions about the animals' treatment, the accuracy of the depiction, and the claims of the narrative. Derek Bousé believes most wildlife films are so highly crafted that they effectively become fictions. Gregg Mitman, on the other hand, believes that nature documentaries' challenges in representing reality are no more complex than they are in other forms of documentary film.

Critics have also questioned whether most popular nature documentaries have positive educational value. Certainly viewers may easily miss a conservationist message. Steve Irwin was a vocal conservationist, but after he was stung to death by a stingray, fans killed and mutilated sting rays up and down the Australian coastline. Bill McKibben charges that when programs show close-ups of endangered species, they communicate the opposite message—there are plenty of cheetahs, look at them! They also create expectations that animals in their own natural setting are in constant dramatic motion. Veteran "blue-chip" documentary producer David Attenborough once said that a program "about a jungle where nothing happens is not really what you turned the television set on to see." Such programs only take a tiny sliver of the animal life—the big mammals, mostly—on the planet seriously. "The upshot of a nature education by television is a deep fondness for certain species and a deep lack of understanding of systems, or of the policies that destroy those systems," McKibben argues.

The global warming crisis may stimulate a trend in nature documentaries to focus not only on animals but on the systems that sustain life and on human beings' role in affecting the system. The field has already evolved considerably. Certainly the casual cruelty and fakery of early nature documentaries would be anathema today.

As nature documentaries fill entire new channels and categories in television's sprawling landscape, they will continue to chronicle, whether deliberately or not, our relationship with our environment. The health of the subgenre is now intimately linked with the health of the global ecosystem.

Chapter 3
Conclusion

The documentary form has evolved with technological possibilities. The advent of sound, color, and 16mm all transformed the way that filmmakers could capture reality and tell stories. The advent of video dramatically changed who could capture reality and expanded the range of people telling stories. IMAX and high-definition technologies brought new spectacle to our screens. Digitization and the Internet once again modify and transfigure possibilities and opportunities. They have made possible mail-order video rental, digital video recorders, broadband television and cell phone movies.

None of these changes made long-form documentary obsolete. Rather, they invested that genre with even more value. Films such as Jehane Noujaim's *Control Room* (three months with Al Jazeera news channel during the beginning of the Iraq war) and Morgan Spurlock's *Super Size Me* (about obesity and fast food) won increased legitimacy from their festival and theatrical achievements in 2004. The market value for high-end spectacle increased, as the growth of IMAX production demonstrated.

These changes have made it possible, however, to imagine documentary on a far wider continuum. Human rights video segments and mini-docs, for example, can be used to spur a Web viewer's commitment, as the organizations WITNESS and OneWorld TV demonstrate. Nongovernmental organizations everywhere can create video for their members, donors, and constituencies, either on their own or with documentary production firms. Young people can produce video of any length, for any purpose, on their own, or with professionals.

Long-form, amateur, and Internet video can all be combined in the same project. The 2004 Video Letters project in the Balkans, executed by the Dutch team Eric van den Broek and Katarina Rejger, facilitated exchanges of video letters among people whose ties had been broken by war. The makers created half-hour television episodes chronicling the interaction and traveled throughout the Balkans with an Internet-equipped van, allowing people to connect with long-lost friends and acquaintances.

Many political movements and organizations have employed documentaries in their causes. Indians in Mexico who joined the Zapatista movement—which announced itself as the Zapatista Army of Liberation (EZLN) to the world in 1993 via the Internet—partnered with international activists to produce videos about their lives and struggle. The videos have been seen in community and religious organizations as well as on the Internet. Young people attracted to the antiglobalization movement have made films witnessing their demonstrations and proclaiming revolutionary intentions, including Big Mouth Media's *Fourth World War* (2004). With small-format cameras, Chinese villagers have documented their outrage at government land confiscation for development projects and attracted international attention.

New technologies do not, of course, solve old problems of truthfulness. The notorious documentary *Loose Change*, a recitation of discredited conspiracy theories about the September 11, 2001, terrorist attacks, is still viewed regularly on the Internet. LonelyGirl15's video blog entries on YouTube, featuring a cloistered religious teen's first daring steps toward rebellion, attracted a huge fan base before a group of artists admitted it was all fiction.

New technologies vastly increase the volume of production under the rubric of documentary. This volume may create new subgenres or may eventually force rethinking. When political operatives, fourth graders, and product marketers all make downloadable documentaries, will we redraw parameters around what we mean by "documentary"?

As we have seen, the genre of documentary is defined by the tension between the claim to truthfulness and the need to select and represent the reality one wants to share. Documentaries are a set of choices—about subject matter, about the forms of expression, about the point of view, about the story line, about the target audience.

While it may seem obvious, these definitions have also been obscured in much debate about documentary. Documentary's founders—Flaherty, Grierson, and Vertov—did not so much articulate the tension driving documentary as exhibit it. Each one of them promised access to reality through art, without explaining at what point artistic license broke the implicit contract with the viewer. New technologies, such as 16mm, have regularly been trumpeted as ways out of the quandary, but they only created more ways to explore it. Applying high journalistic standards can work toward accuracy, but those standards do not resolve the problem that a documentary always represents rather than just showing reality.

Documentarians will continue to wrestle productively with questions such as: How does a filmmaker responsibly represent reality? What truths will be told? Why are they important, and to whom? What is the filmmaker's responsibility to and relationship with the subjects of the work? Who gets the opportunity to make documentaries, how are they seen, and under what constraints?

Filmmakers will work with the tools at hand. These include the formal conventions that register good faith, accuracy, and unique presence to a viewer, conventions that can be anything from a sonorous narrator to a shaky camera. They include expectations that viewers bring with them from established subgenres and include the participation of authorities and celebrities, and the imprimatur of organizations that viewers trust.

Makers will also benefit from studying the struggles of past documentarians to work in good faith, whether it is the political passion of a Joris Ivens or a Barbara Kopple, the cross-cultural pursuits of a Jean Rouch, the empathic explorations of an Allan King, the historical mission of a Henry Hampton.

The problem of how to represent reality will continue to be worth wrestling with, because the documentary says, "This really happened, and it was important enough to show you. Watch it." The importance of documentary may be in public affairs or celebrity-driven entertainment. It may be important for fourteen-year-old skateboarders or residents of one apartment building; it may be important until the end of the month or the end of the semester or the end of time. Documentary makes connections, grounded in real life experience that is undeniable because you can see and hear it.

A note on history and scholarship

This book is informed by a substantial body of scholarship, much of it but by no means all created by academics. This note sketches the evolution of documentary scholarship, in the hopes that those captivated by the challenges of documentary may also contribute to its understanding.

Most filmmakers are too busy making their work to describe it, much less archive it and locate it in a context. Journalists rarely have the luxury of historical research and comparative knowledge of the field (with striking exceptions such as J. Hoberman, Ruby Rich, Jonathan Rosenbaum, and Stuart Klawans); academic work is, therefore, a key resource for documentary. Scholarship identifies important creators and trends, keeps a record of what has gone before, and also sets the agenda for what we think are the main issues or problems in documentary. It is an ongoing and fluid process.

Makers were the first recorders of documentary history, though, and they were predictably biased. For decades, the most prolific and the most widely circulated writers were Griersonians. Leading writer, teacher, and filmmaker Paul Rotha argued that documentary was "instruction for the awakening of civic consciousness among the public," and Rotha's writing was part of the missionary work he did to raise that consciousness. His *Documentary Film: The Use of the Film Medium to Interpret Creatively and in Social Terms the Life of the People as it Exists in Reality* was translated into several languages and widely used in courses. He recounted history—focused only on Europe—as background to his teaching of film production. Learn, he counseled, from the close observation of the romantic Flaherty; from the aesthetic experiments of continental Europeans such as Cavalcanti, Ruttman, and Ivens; from the reportorial passion of Vertov and the propagandistic techniques of Eisenstein and of Grierson, in order to make your socially influential work.

Historical narrative

The definitive narrative of documentary history was established in 1971 by Erik Barnouw. The Dutch-born American scholar, filmmaker, and curator undertook the task of writing a truly international history of documentary, titled, simply, *Documentary*. His task, undertaken while teaching at Columbia University, took him to more than a score of nations worldwide, including Japan, India, Egypt, the Soviet Union, and countries in

Eastern Europe as well as Western European film-producing countries. With a broad humanist vision and healthy curiosity, he asked himself what conditions create the possibilities for certain kinds of work (i.e., propaganda, or avant-garde art film), and he focused on leading and influential figures.

In Barnouw's resulting unpretentious and authoritative social history, Flaherty, Grierson, and Vertov were no longer warring factions to be judged but historical innovators differently setting history in motion. He used charismatic creators as guides through the history, exemplifying eras and approaches. The book begins with early experiments in nonfiction at the origins of cinema. Barnouw's founding fathers (the founding was male-dominated, although women provided critically important support in production, editing, and marketing) include Flaherty, the Explorer; Dziga Vertov, the Reporter; young Joris Ivens, the Painter; and Grierson, the Advocate.

The narrative tracks the growth of the powerful advocacy impulse in the early work of German fascist documentarian Leni Riefenstahl, the New Deal work of Pare Lorentz in the United States, leftist filmmaking in 1930s Japan, and the work of the British documentary movement, which culminated in the wartime propaganda of World War II. The book describes use of documentary film in the postwar period as poetry, as history, ethnography, and advocacy. It charts the rise of the sponsored documentary and the TV documentary. An international movement of dissent also develops new expressive techniques. The observational fly-on-the-wall approach exemplified by artists such as Richard Leacock, Albert and David Maysles, Frederick Wiseman, and Allan King is compared with the more provocative cinema verité approach practiced by artists worldwide. The narrative ends with a range of dissident film movements: underground films in the new Soviet empire, protest films against the American war in Vietnam, and films protesting industrial growth in Japan, among others.

Unsentimentally and with a wealth of specifics, Barnouw portrayed documentary makers overall as voices of freedom, conviction, and engagement with the world. He showed them exploring the medium to tell stories neglected by the ever-more-powerful mainstream media, which he had earlier analyzed in a three-volume history of television. *Documentary* was immediately used in film studies classes, which were growing rapidly in popularity. In the same time period, others also produced popular texts developed out of classroom use and production mentoring. Lewis Jacobs created a valuable anthology of writings on documentary, for example. He organized it more or less chronologically, with such themes as innovation (the founder era), conservatism (the postwar moment), and engagement (cinema verité). Richard Barsam developed a framework that looked at documentary as an art within a longer aesthetic tradition of realism, and which also took a broad range of expression into consideration, in *Nonfiction Film: A Critical History*. Jack Ellis, who had worked with Grierson, published *The Documentary Idea*, which focused on English-language social documentary and unabashedly showed his fondness for Grierson; he later updated it with Betsy McLane. However, the broad geographical and aesthetic range and limpid clarity of Barnouw was unmatched by any other synthetic historian.

Analytical scholarship

Scholarship about documentaries developed as cinema studies, growing out of literature departments, and some students became professors in the discipline. The origins of the field skewed scholarly research toward the analytical focus on texts typical of literary scholars—with the text in this case being the film. As the academic field of cultural studies—the study of the formation of culture, with particular attention to conditions of production and reception—grew, so did studies of how film movements developed and how films were received and used.

Academics have extensively explored the complexities behind documentary's seemingly simple claim to truthfulness about the real world. Their close readings of films have parsed exactly how filmmakers achieve the illusion of transparent revelation of truth; they have often brought a rich body of biographical and historical knowledge to their close readings as well. In addition, they have challenged and reexamined the reputation and role of foundational figures, particularly those of Grierson and Flaherty.

In this genre, academics have developed their own categories within which to understand and critique the work of documentarians. Categorization lays the groundwork for them to interpret and analyze the work; such categories have value only as they help explain how documentaries work, and as they continue to be invented. Scholarly categories differ sharply from the categories used in the business marketplace, where subject areas (history, wildlife, science, children's) dominate. They focus on the *techniques* filmmakers use to represent reality and thus put the problem of representation in such a way that convinces viewers it is not representation at all, but reality. Bill Nichols, for example, described four ways of addressing the viewer in documentary, each with different implications for claims to truthfulness: expository (i.e., a voice-of-god narrator); observational (such as the Maysles brothers' work); interactive (oral histories and interviews and the like); and reflexive (work that comments on its own form, such as that of Vertov or the film *The Ax Fight*). Nichols and others critiqued and added to these categories; Keith Beattie added reconstructive (docudrama) and observation-entertainment (reality TV) to the list. Michael Renov described four functional modes of documentaries: recording, persuading, analyzing, and expressing.

Many academics and scholars have dedicated themselves to chronicling and analyzing advocacy and activist documentaries. This reflects in part the historic role of documentarians, so well identified by Barnouw, as voices of dissent and criticism. It also shows a liberal tilt in the academic community as well as in the living center of documentary production in the 1970s and early 1980s when the first wave of documentary studies scholars were completing their first work. This focus on activism has been particularly well represented in the Visible Evidence book series. For instance, work has been done on AIDS activist documentaries from the 1980s on in the United States; feminist, gay and lesbian documentaries, African American documentaries, and "guerrilla" or alternative and oppositional documentaries.

There are many ways of asking why and how documentaries differ from fiction film, given that they share so many techniques. William Guynn, drawing on theory developed for fiction films, has argued that documentary film is less satisfying than fiction, because it fails to give the viewer the same unrecognized return of the repressed—the promise of fantastic unity and integration. Postmodernist analysts challenge documentary's use of psychological realism (much the same as in fiction film) to represent reality. Realism, in their analysis, works merely to obscure the ideology of bourgeois culture. Nichols argues that documentaries that play with the viewer's expectation for transparency and truth reflect more creatively the multiple perspectives of postmodern life. Meanwhile, Brian Winston states that in an age of endless digital manipulation and aggressive viewer intervention, documentarians cannot claim either scientific accuracy or paternalistic right to lecture but must acknowledge that they are merely a speaker among speakers. Cognitive theorists such as Noël Carroll respond that human beings reasonably accurately interpret the data from the world around them, including that from the screens they watch. The illusion of reality, they argue, is not necessarily disempowering.

Emerging areas

Documentary scholarship is still developing, and there are fruitful potential areas of growth. English-speaking scholars, for example, have typically drawn little on international scholarship on documentary, although the reverse is not necessarily true. The

Yamagata film festival in Japan has vigorously fostered international exchange of scholarship with its online *Documentary Box*. There have been some impressive exceptions to English-language parochialism as well, such as the work of Julianne Burton and Michael Chanan on Latin American documentary and Markus Nornes on Japanese documentary.

Most cinema studies scholars know little of the business of documentary distribution and are little interested in the most popular kinds of documentary. They have focused primarily on independent production and films for general audiences, and on dissident and art-house works. They typically leave speculation about the effects of formulaic and sponsored documentary—where authorship is often much harder to track— to sociologists and other social scientists who study media effects and who often have no particular knowledge of documentary form and tradition.

And yet documentaries made for clients ("sponsored" documentaries) and those formulaic documentaries shown on television are important and growing facets of documentary production, both of which are usually viewers' first experiences of documentary. Sponsored and formulaic TV films also often subsidize independent work, since this part of the business provides steady work for documentarians. Indeed, in some developing countries, sponsored work keeps the entire film sector alive in between big projects. Looking at the intersections between sponsored and independent work could provide a better understanding of how documentary evolves.

Because so little research has been done on sponsored documentaries, we know little about an area that surely accounts for the majority of film productions. Organizations now use documentaries for conventions, board meetings, presentations, sales campaigns, and in strategic campaigns aimed at schoolchildren, AIDS patients, or employees learning to avoid sexual harassment and the like. Sponsored filmmaking, both corporate and government, has also generated rich archival resources for filmmakers.

Formulaic documentaries made as lowbrow entertainment have not caught many researchers' attention, but they may as the popularity of the genre grows. Cinema studies scholars eventually began studying genres such as the noir film and "the genius of the system," as Thomas Schatz called it, of movie studios; the example would be well applied to the work of documentary-factories such as Discovery Communications.

As entertainment documentaries grow in importance, we can expect to see scholars exploring these subgenres, their structures, strategies of representation, and appeal. Performance documentaries in music and comedy, "making of" documentaries, extreme sports documentaries, television series such as how-tos, makeovers, cooking and other series, and docusoaps all build not only upon earlier by innovative documentarians but also condition the marketplace and viewers' expectations. Early work, some of which is listed in Further Reading, has been done on rockumentaries, such as D A Pennebaker's cinema verité classic *Dont Look Back* (1967) about a Bob Dylan tour, Martin Scorsese's *The Last Waltz* (1978) on The Band, and Jonathan Demme's 1984 *Stop Making Sense*, featuring the Talking Heads. Attention to more popular work will also engage scholars more fully with the economic realities of an art form bound tightly to commercial mass media; and we will learn more, through these means, about how economic conditions shape expression.

Other changes in documentary expression may well provoke academic activity. Burgeoning production in advocacy documentary and growing popularity of documentaries on timely topics may stimulate academic work on standards and ethics in the field. The growth in participatory media may stimulate more interdisciplinary work, as sociologists, anthropologists, communications scholars, political scientists, information scientists, and film scholars each seek to understand the phenomenon. Scholarship will continue to change our understanding of documentary, and it will reflect a creative engagement between the interests of academics and the practices of documentarians.

One Hundred Great Documentaries

These documentaries have been widely seen and discussed, and have been in many cases at the center of controversies; in other cases they have provided valuable teaching resources. They are all accessible for renting or buying for your private collection. You can use the index to this book and other books mentioned in the references, imdb.com, your local library, Netflix, Google, and the Library of Congress to find out more about why these films have attracted attention and esteem. Viewing this collection will set you up nicely with a context to watch your latest favorite, argue with this list, and build your own top one hundred.

Nanook of the North, 1922
Grass, 1925
Berlin, Symphony of a Great City, 1927
The Fall of the Romanov Dynasty, 1927
Man with a Movie Camera, 1929
Rain, 1929
Land without Bread (Las Hurdes), 1932
Man of Aran, 1934
Song of Ceylon, 1934
Triumph of the Will, 1934
Night Mail, 1936
The Plow that Broke the Plains, 1936
Spanish Earth, 1937
Power and the Land, 1939–40
Listen to Britain, 1942
Why We Fight, 1942
Battle of San Pietro, 1945
Farrebique, 1946
Maîtres Fou, Les (Crazy Masters), 1955
Night and Fog, 1955

Documentary Film

Tire Dié, 1958
Primary, 1960
Chronicle of a Summer, 1961
Mothlight, 1963
Battle of Culloden, 1964
Tokyo Olympiad, 1965
Dont Look Back, 1967
Titicut Follies, 1967
Warrendale, 1967
Hour of the Furnaces, 1968
Salesman, 1968
High School, 1969
Sorrow and the Pity, 1969
Selling of the Pentagon, 1971
World at War, 1973
Hearts and Minds, 1974
Ax Fight, 1975
Battle of Chile, 1975–79
The Wedding Camels, 1976
Harlan County USA, 1976
How the Myth Was Made, 1978
The Last Waltz, 1978
With Babies and Banners, 1978
Trobriand Cricket, 1979
The Life and Times of Rosie the Riveter, 1980
N!ai: The Story of a !Kung Woman, 1980
Garden of Earthly Delights, 1981
Atomic Café, 1982
Burden of Dreams, 1982
Sans Soleil (Sunless), 1982
First Contact, 1983
When the Mountains Tremble, 1983
Cabra Marcado para Morrer (Twenty Years Later, a.k.a. A Man Listed to Die), 1984
Shoah, 1985
From the Pole to the Equator, 1986
Handsworth Songs, 1986
Sherman's March, 1986
Eyes on the Prize, 1987–90
Cane Toads, 1988
The Emperor's Naked Army Marches On, 1988
The Thin Blue Line, 1988
Roger & Me, 1989
Tongues Untied, 1989
Body Beautiful, 1990
The Civil War, 1990
Paris Is Burning, 1990
Allah, Tantou, 1991
Afrique, Je Te Plumerai, 1992
Lumumba, Death of a Prophet, 1992
The War Room, 1993
The Wonderful, Horrible Life of Leni Riefenstahl, 1993
Hoop Dreams, 1994
Celluloid Closet, 1995
Taking Pictures, 1996
4 Little Girls, 1997
Chile, Obstinate Memory, 1997
42 Up, 1998
What Farocki Taught, 1998
Cinéma vérité, 1999
Gleaners and I, 2000
Stranger with a Camera, 2000
Dogtown and Z-Boys, 2001

Fighter, 2001
Winged Migration, 2001
Amandla!, 2002
Bus 174, 2002
The Day I Will Never Forget, 2002
Rivers and Tides, 2002
Checkpoint, 2003
Fog of War, 2003
Control Room, 2004
Fahrenheit 9/11, 2004
From the Ikpeng Children to the World, 2004
The New Americans, 2004
Super Size Me, 2004
Tintin and I, 2004
Video Letters, 2004
A Decent Factory, 2005
Three Rooms of Melancholia, 2005
An Inconvenient Truth, 2006

Further Reading and Viewing

I have included here the most important texts I consulted in writing the book (in the case of prolific authors not all their books are referenced). Grant and Sloniowski, Warren and Izod, et al. are all essay collections featuring authors I have referred to in the text. The place where I and almost everybody else started was, of course, Erik Barnouw.

Films

McLaren, Les, and Annie Stiven. *Taking Pictures*. First Run Icarus, 1996.

Müller, Ray. *The Wonderful Horrible Life of Leni Riefenstahl*. Kino on Video, 1998.

Stoney, George. *How the Myth Was Made*. Available on the Home Vision DVD of *Man of Aran*, 1978.

Wintonick, Peter. *Cinema vérité: Defining the Moment*. National Film Board of Canada, 1999.

Print

Aitken, Ian. *Film and Reform: John Grierson and the Documentary Film Movement*. London: Routledge, 1990.

——. *The Documentary Film Movement: An Anthology*. Edinburgh: Edinburgh University Press, 1998.

Alexander, William. *Film on the Left: American Documentary Film from 1931 to 1942*. Princeton, NJ: Princeton University Press, 1981.

Anderson, Joseph L., and Donald Richie. *The Japanese Film: Art and Industry*. Princeton, NJ: Princeton University Press, 1982.

Aufderheide, Patricia. *The Daily Planet: A Critic on the Capitalist Culture Beat*. Minneapolis: University of Minnesota Press, 2000.

Aufderheide, Patricia, and Peter Jaszi, *Untold Stories: Creative Consequences of the Rights Clearance Culture for Documentary Filmmakers*. Washington, DC: Center for Social Media, American University, 2004.

Barnouw, Erik. *Tube of Plenty: The Evolution of American Television*. New York: Oxford University Press, 1982.

———. *Documentary: A History of the Non-fiction Film*. New York: Oxford University Press, 1993.

———. *Media Marathon: A Twentieth-Century Memoir*. Durham, NC: Duke University Press, 1996.

Barsam, Richard. *Nonfiction Film: A Critical History*. New York: Dutton, 1973.

Beattie, Keith. *Documentary Screens: Non-fiction Film and Television*. New York: Palgrave Macmillan, 2004.

Benson, Thomas W., and Carolyn Anderson. *Reality Fictions: The Films of Frederick Wiseman*. Carbondale, IL: Southern Illinois University Press, 1989.

Bernard, Sheila Curran. *Documentary Storytelling for Film and Videomakers*. Boston: Focal Press, 2004.

Bluem, A. William. *Documentary in American Television: Form, Function [and] Method*. Hastings House, 1965.

Bousé, Derek. *Wildlife Films*. Philadelphia: University of Pennsylvania Press, 2000.

Boyle, Deirdre. *Subject to Change: Guerrilla Television Revisited*. New York: Oxford University Press, 1997.

Burton, Julianne. *The Social Documentary in Latin America*. Pittsburgh, PA: University of Pittsburgh Press, 1990.

Campbell, Richard. *60 Minutes and the News: A Mythology for Middle America*. Urbana: University of Illinois Press, 1991.

Campbell, Russell. *Cinema Strikes Back: Radical Filmmaking in the United States, 1930–1942*. Ann Arbor, MI: UMI Research Press, 1982.

Carey, James W. *Communication as Culture: Essays on Media and Society*. London: Unwin Hyman, 1989.

Carroll, Noël. *Engaging the Moving Image*. New Haven, CT: Yale University Press, 2003.

Chanan, Michael. *Cuban Cinema*. Minneapolis: University of Minnesota Press, 2003.

Culbert, David, Richard E. Wood, et al. *Film and Propaganda in America: A Documentary History*. Westport, CT: Greenwood Press, 1990.

Cunningham, Megan. *The Art of the Documentary*. Berkeley: New Riders, 2005.

Delmar, Rosalind. *Joris Ivens: 50 years of Film-making*. London: Educational Advisory Service, British Film Institute, 1979.

Dewey, John. *The Public and Its Problems*. New York: H. Holt and Company, 1927.

Doherty, Thomas. *Cold War, Cool Medium: Television, McCarthyism, and American Culture*. New York: Columbia University Press, 2003.

Eaton, Mick. *Anthropology, Reality, Cinema: The Films of Jean Rouch*. London: British Film Institute, 1979.

Edgerton, Gary R. *Ken Burns's America*. New York: Palgrave, 2001.

Ellis, Jack C. *John Grierson: Life, Contributions, Influence*. Carbondale, IL: Southern Illinois University Press, 2000.

Elsaesser, Thomas. *Harun Farocki: Working on the Sight-lines*. Amsterdam: Amsterdam University Press, 2004.

Evans, Gary. *John Grierson and the National Film Board: The Politics of Wartime Propaganda*. Toronto: University of Toronto Press, 1984.

Feldman, Seth. *Allan King: Filmmaker*. Toronto: Toronto International Film Festival, 2002.

Ginsburg, Faye D., Lila Abu-Lughod, et al. *Media Worlds: Anthropology on New Terrain*. Berkeley: University of California Press, 2002.

Grant, Barry, and Jeannette Sloniowski. *Documenting the Documentary: Close Readings of Documentary Film and Video*. Detroit: Wayne State University Press, 1998.

Guynn, William. *A Cinema of Nonfiction*. Madison, NJ: Fairleigh Dickinson University Press, 1990.

Hall, Jeanne. "Realism as a style in cinema vérité: a critical analysis of *Primary*." *Cinema Journal* 30, no. 4 (1991): 38–45.

Halleck, DeeDee. *Hand-held Visions: The Impossible Possibilities of Community Media*. New York: Fordham University Press, 2002.

Henaut, Dorothy. "Video Stories from the Dawn of Time." *Visual Anthropology Review* 7, no. 2 (1991): 85–101.

Hirsch, Marianne. *Family Frames: Photography, Narrative, and Postmemory*. Cambridge, MA: Harvard University Press, 1997.

Holmlund, Chris, and Cynthia Fuchs. *Between the Sheets, in the Streets: Queer, Lesbian, and Gay Documentary*. Minneapolis: University of Minnesota Press, 1997.

Izod, John, R. W. Kilborn, et al. *From Grierson to the Docu-soap: Breaking the Boundaries*. Hadleigh, Essex, UK: University of Luton Press, 2000.

Jacobs, Lewis. *The Documentary Tradition, from Nanook to Woodstock*. New York: Hopkinson and Blake, 1971.

Juhasz, Alexandra. *Women of Vision: Histories in Feminist Film and Video*. Minneapolis: University of Minnesota Press, 2001.

Juhasz, Alexandra, and Catherine Saalfield. *AIDS TV: Identity, Community, and Alternative Video*. Durham, NC: Duke University Press, 1995.

King, John. *Magical Reels: A History of Cinema in Latin America*. London: Verso, in association with the Latin American Bureau, 1990.

Klotman, Phyllis, and Janet Cutler. *Struggles for Representation: African American Documentary Film and Video*. Bloomington: Indiana University Press, 1999.

Leyda, Jay. *Films Beget Films*. New York: Hill and Wang, 1964.

——. *Kino: A History of the Russian and Soviet Film*. Princeton, NJ: Princeton University Press, 1983.

MacDonald, Scott. *The Garden in the Machine: A Field Guide to Independent Films about Place*. Berkeley: University of California Press, 2002.

——. *A Critical Cinema 4: Interviews with Independent Filmmakers*. Berkeley: University of California Press, 2005.

MacDougall, David, and Lucien Taylor. *Transcultural Cinema*. Princeton, NJ: Princeton University Press, 1998.

Mamber, Stephen. *Cinema Verité in America: Studies in Uncontrolled Documentary*. Cambridge, MA: MIT Press, 1974.

Marx, Leo. *The Machine in the Garden: Technology and the Pastoral Ideal in America*. New York: Oxford University Press, 2000.

Matthieson, Donald. "Persuasive History: A Critical Comparison of Television's Victory at Sea and The World at War." *History Teacher* 25, no. 2 (1992): 239–51.

McEnteer, James. *Shooting the Truth: The Rise of American Political Documentaries*. Westport, CT: Praeger Publishers, 2006.

McKibben, Bill. *The Age of Missing Information*. New York: Random House, 1992.

Michaels, Eric. *Bad Aboriginal Art: Tradition, Media, and Technological Horizons*. Minneapolis: University of Minnesota Press, 1994.

Mitman, Gregg. *Reel Nature: America's Romance with Wildlife on Films*. Cambridge, MA: Harvard University Press, 1999.

Moran, James M. *There's No Place like Home Video*. Minneapolis: University of Minnesota Press, 2002.

Nelson, Joyce. *The Colonized Eye: Rethinking the Grierson Legend*. Toronto: Between the Lines, 1988.

Nichols, Bill. *Representing Reality: Issues and Concepts in Documentary*. Bloomington: Indiana University Press, 1991.

——. *Blurred Boundaries: Questions of Meaning in Contemporary Culture*. Bloomington: Indiana University Press, 1994.

Nornes, Markus. *Japanese Documentary Film: The Meiji Era through Hiroshima*. Minneapolis: University of Minnesota Press, 2003.

O'Connell, P.J. *Robert Drew and the Development of Cinema Verité in America*. Carbondale, IL: Southern Illinois University Press, 1992.

Orbanz, Eve. *Journey to a Legend and Back*. Berlin: Verlag Volker Spiess, 1977.

Rabiger, Michael. *Directing the Documentary*. Boston: Focal Press, 2004.

Raphael, Chad. *Investigated Reporting: Muckrakers, Regulators, and the Struggle over Television Documentary*. Carbondale, IL: University of Illinois Press, 2005.

Rees, A. L. *A History of Experimental Film and Video: From Canonical Avant-Garde to Contemporary British Practice*. London: BFI Publishing, 1999.

Reeves, Nicholas. *The Power of Film Propaganda: Myth or Reality?* London: Cassell, 1999.

Renov, Michael. *Theorizing Documentary*. London: Routledge, 1993.

——. *The Subject of Documentary*. Minneapolis: University of Minnesota Press, 2004.

Rich, B. Ruby. *Chick Flicks: Theories and Memories of the Feminist Film Movement*. Durham, NC: Duke University Press, 1998.

Roscoe, Jane, and Craig Hight. *Faking It: Mock-documentary and the Subversion of Factuality*. Manchester, UK: Manchester University Press, 2001.

Rosenthal, Alan. *New Challenges for Documentary*. Berkeley: University of California Press, 1988.

Rosteck, Thomas. *"See It Now" Confronts McCarthyism: Television Documentary and the Politics of Representation.* Tuscaloosa: University of Alabama Press, 1994.

Roth, Lorna. *Something New in the Air: The Story of First Peoples Television Broadcasting in Canada.* Montreal: McGill-Queen's University Press, 2005.

Rotha, Paul. *Documentary Film: The Use of the Film Medium to Interpret Creatively and in Social Terms the Life of the People as It Exists in Reality.* New York: Hastings House, 1963.

Rotha, Paul, and Jay Ruby. *Robert J. Flaherty, a Biography.* Philadelphia: University of Pennsylvania Press, 1983.

Rothman, William. *Documentary Film Classics.* New York: Cambridge University Press, 1997.

Rouch, Jean, and Steven Feld. *Ciné-ethnography.* Minneapolis: University of Minnesota Press, 2003.

Ruby, Jay. *Picturing Culture: Explorations of Film & Anthropology.* Chicago: University of Chicago Press, 2000.

Sato, Tadao. *Currents in Japanese Cinema: Essays.* Tokyo: Kodansha International, 1982.

Schoots, Hans. *Joris Ivens: Living Dangerously.* Amsterdam: Amsterdam University Press, 2000.

Stam, Robert. *Film Theory: An Introduction.* Oxford: Blackwell, 2000.

Sussex, Elizabeth. *The Rise and Fall of British Documentary: The Story of the Film Movement Founded by John Grierson.* Berkeley: University of California Press, 1975.

Vaughan, Dai. *For Documentary: Twelve Essays.* Berkeley: University of California Press, 1999.

Vertov, Dziga, and Annette Michelson. *Kino-eye: The Writings of Dziga Vertov.* Berkeley: University of California Press, 1984.

Video nas aldeias (Video in the Villages). *Um olhar indigena.* São Paulo: Banco do Brasil, 2004.

Charles Warren, *Beyond Document: Essays on Nonfiction Film.* Lebanon, NH: University Press of New England for Wesleyan University Press, 1996.

Waugh, Thomas. *"Show Us Life": Toward a History and Aesthetics of the Committed Documentary.* Lanham, MD: Scarecrow Press, 1984.

Wees, William C. *Light Moving in Time: Studies in the Visual Aesthetics of Avant-Garde Film.* Berkeley: University of California Press, 1992.

Welsh, James Michael. *Peter Watkins: A Guide to References and Resources*. Boston: G. K. Hall, 1986.

Winston, Brian. *Claiming the Real: The Griersonian Documentary and Its Legitimations*. London: British Film Institute, 1995.

Worth, Sol, and John Adair. *Through Navajo Eyes: An Exploration in Film Communication and Anthropology*. Albuquerque: University of New Mexico Press, 1997.

Zimmermann, Patricia. *Reel Families: A Social History of Amateur Film*. Bloomington: Indiana University Press, 1995.

Index

A

Abrash, Barbara, x
Achkar, David, 102
Adair, John, 106–7
advocacy film. *See also* third cinema
  cinema verité and, 87
  collectives of, 82
  CP and, 79–81
  Flaherty, Robert, influence on, 86
  Godard group for, 82
  Godard influence on, 86
  government propaganda
    documentary *v.*, 77–78
  Great Depression and, 79
  Grierson, John, influence on, 86
  Ivens and, 79
  legacy of, 87–91
  Marker group for, 82
  Moore *v.*, 78
  Stoney and, 87–88
  Vertov influence on, 86
*Afrique, Je Te Plumerai (Africa,
  I Will Fleece You)*, 102
Akomfrah, John, 101–2
Allah, Tantou, 102
Allen, Woody, 88
Alvarez, Santiago, 83
American Civil Liberties
  Union, 77
American Masters, 95–96
An American Family, 55
Anderson, Carolyn, 53
Anderson, Lindsay, 46
  on cinema verité, 52–53
Anderson, Robin, 109
Anderson, Thom, 15–16
Andy Warhol, 96
Anger, Kenneth, 16
An Inconvenient Truth, 7–8,
  122, *123*
Anka, Paul, 47
Anstey, Edgar, 34
À Propos de Nice, 15
Apta, Jan, 51
art films
  conventions *v.*, 14, 17–18
  optic experiments of, 16
  sound experiments of, 17–18
Asch, Tim, 110–11
The Atomic Café, 75
Attenborough, David, 124
Australian National Film
  Board, 36
The Ax Fight, 110–11, 132

B

Babakiueria, 13
Bagwell, Orlando, x–xi
Banks and the Poor, 59
Bar-Lev, Amir, 104
Barnouw, Erik, x, 50, 73–74,
  129–32
Barsam, Richard, 131
*The Battle of Chile (La Batalla
  de Chile)*, 85, *103*
  Chile, Obstinate Memory and, 104
  impact of, 90
The Battle of San Piedro, 73
The Battle of the Somme, 65
Beattie, Keith, 132
Beauviola, Jean-Pierre, 46
Belson, Jordan, 16
Benson, Thomas, 53
Berlin: Symphony of a Great City,
  14–15

Best in Show, 14
Big Cat, 121
Binford, Mira, 104
Bing, Wang, 45
Birri, Fernando, 83–84
Birth of a Nation, 27
Black Audio Collective, 101
Blank, Les, x, 106
Blood of the Beasts (Le sang des bêtes), 46
Bluem, A. William, 53
Blue Planet, 120
Blue Vinyl, 8
Body Beautiful, 102
Border War, 90
Borinage, 79, 90–91
Bousé, Derek, 123
Brakhage, Stan, 16
Brandeis, Louis, 77
Brault, Michael, 53
Brave New Films, 6–7, 90
Britten, Benjamin, 34
Broderick, Peter, 21
Broomfield, Nick, 55
Brottman, Mikita, 96
Bumming in Beijing, 87
Buñuel, Luis, 13
Burns, Ken, 13
  on *The Civil War*, 94
  The Civil War by, 93–94
  critical opinion on work of, 94
Burton, Julianne, 134
Bus 174, 8–9

C

Cabra Marcado para Morrer (Twenty Years Later, a.k.a. A Man Listed to Die), 102, 104
Cadillac Desert, 105
Canadian National Film Board, 18, 36, 38, 47–48, 75, 115
Cane Toads, 122
Cannibal Tours, 114

Capra , Frank, 70, 72–73
  on government propaganda documentary, 74
career beginnings
  of Flaherty, Robert, 27
  of Grierson, John, 32–33
  of Vertov, 39–40
Carey, James, 5
Carroll, Noël
  on cinema verité, 53
  on documentary and realism, 133
Cavalcanti, Alberto, 15
CBS Reports, 58
  significant results from, 60
Celsius 41.11, 78
Chagnon, Napoleon, 110–11
Challenge for Change, 47, 49
Chanan, Michael, 134
Chang, 107
Checkpoint, 9
Cheiro de Pequi (The Smell of the Pequi Fruit), 115, 116
Chequerboard, 58
The Chicago Maternity Center Story, 88
Chicano!, 99–100
Chile, Obstinate Memory, 103, 104
Chronicle of a Summer, 51, 112
Cinema-Eye (Kino-Glaz), 41–42
cinema verité
  advocacy film and, 87
  in Britain, 46
  in Canada, 46–47, 49
  controversy with, 51–52
  corporate struggles with, 47
  ethics and, 54–55
  evolution of, 45–49
  in France, 46
  present state of, 55
  public affairs documentary and, 63
  style of, 44–45
  in United States, 46–47
city symphony films, 14–16
The Civil War, 93–94

Close-Up!, 58
Communist Party (CP)
   advocacy film and, 79–81
   The Spanish Earth and, 80
Connelly, Bob, 109
Control Room, 125
conventions
   art films v., 14, 17–18
   business realities and, 18
   documentary, 11–12
   of ethnographic film, 108–9
   of public affairs documentary, 62–63
   satire of, 13
Cooper, Merian C., 107
Coutinho, Eduardo, 102, 104
Cowell, Adrian, 60
Coyote, Peter, 90–91
CP. *See* Communist Party
Cree Hunters of the Mistassini, 115
critical opinion
   on work of Burns, 94
   on work of Flaherty, Robert, 31–32
   on work of Grierson, John, 36–37
   on work of Maysles, Albert, 55
   on work of Maysles, David, 55
   on work of public affairs documentary, 63–64
   on work of Vertov, 41
   on work of Wiseman, 53
The Crocodile Hunter, 119
Crumb, 55
Curtis, Adam, 60
Curtis, Edward S., 28
Cutler, R.J., 50

D

Daum, Menachem, 104
Davis, Peter, 53–54
   influential films of, 62
Dead Birds, 108
de Antonio, Emile, 24, 62

Decade of Destruction, 60
The Defense of the United States, 60
Demme, Jonathan, 135
Derrida, 96–97
Dewey, John, 5
Dhrupad, 17
Diamonds in the Snow, 104
Dick, Kirby, 96–97
Disappearing World, 108
docudramas, 23
documentary. *See also* advocacy film; art films; city symphony films; docudramas; ethnographic film; government propaganda documentary; historical documentary; mockumentary; nature documentary; personal diary format; public affairs documentary
   analytical scholarship of, 131–33
   audience expectations with, 2–3
   categorization of, 132
   conventions of, 11–12
   defining, 1–3, 9–10
   evolution of, 125–28
   fiction film v., 2, 12, 133
   forms of, 10–12
   historical texts of, 129–31
   new technologies and, 126–28
   public issues and, 4–9
   reality and, 5, 9–12
   revenues of, 5
   scholarship of, 128–29, 133–36
   terms of, 3–4
   tools of, 10–11
Documentary (Barnouw), 129–31
Documentary Box, 134
Documentary Filmmakers' Statement of Best Practices in Fair Use, 95
Documentary Film: The Use of the Film Medium to Interpret

Creativity and in Social Terms the Life of the People as it Exists in Reality (Rotha), 129
The Documentary Idea (Ellis), 131
Dogtown and Z-Boys, 104
Dont Look Back, 53, 135
Drew, Robert, 46–47
   on documentaries of past, 51
   public affairs documentary and, 63
Drifters, 33
Dziga Vertov group, 82

E

Edgerton, Gary, 94
Eisenstein, Sergi, 42–43
The Eleventh Year, 42
Ellis, Jack, 131
Else, Jon
   on accuracy in film, 105
   ethical concerns of, 22
   story structure and, 12
The Emperor's Naked Army Marches On, 99
End of the Dialogue (Phela-Ndaba), 82
Enthusiasm, 42
The Eternal Jew, 6
ethics
   cinema verité and, 54–55
   controversial approaches and, 23–25
   Else concerns on, 22
   ethnographic film and, 116–17
   Ginsburg on ethnographic film and, 116–17
   government propaganda documentary and, 74–75
   of interviews, 98–99
   nature documentary and, 123–24
   Nicholas and, 22
   public affairs documentary and, 63–64
   reenactment and, 22–23

ethnographic film
   audiences and, 117
   conventions of, 108–9
   defining, 106
   ethics and, 116–17
   Ginsburg on ethics in, 116–17
   indigenous creators in, 114–17
   revenues from, 107
   science and, 109–11
   subject participation in, 113–14
Eyes on the Prize, 99
Eye Spy, 76

F

Fahrenheit 9/11, ix, 1
   Celsius 41.11 v., 78
   propaganda *v.,* 7
The Fall of the Romanov Dynasty, 92–93
Faloni, Luigi, 32
Farocki, Harun, 24
Farrebique, 119
fiction film, documentary *v.,* 2, 12, 133
Field, Connie, 99
Fighter, 104
First Contact, 109
Flaherty, Frances, 31
Flaherty, Robert, 2–3, 108, 127, 129–30, 132
   advocacy film influenced by, 86
   appeal of, 30–31
   artistic choices of, 28, 30
   career beginnings of, 27
   corporate sponsors and, 20
   critical opinion on work of, 31–32
   Grierson, John, influenced by, 33
   Grierson, John, *v.,* 38
   Grierson, John, working with, 34
   legacy of, 32
   on *Nanook of the North,* 28–29
   realism of, 25–26
   Rouch influenced by, 111

The Spanish Earth influenced
by, 80
Stoney influenced by, 30–31
themes of, 29–30
Vertov *v.*, 44
Fog of War, 97
The Ford Foundation, x–xi
Forest of Bliss, 108
Forgács, Peter, 104
The Forgotten Imperial Army, 49
formalism, 26
Forward, Soviet!, 42
Four Corners, 58
Fourth World War, 126
Fox, Beryl, 61
Fragrant Jewel Island, 86
Franju, Georges, 46
Freedom Files, 77
Friendly, Fred, 57
From the Ikpeng Children to the World, 116
From the Pole to the Equator, 118
Frontline, 59–60
funding
  corporate, 20–21
  direct sale, 21–22
  government, 18–20

G

Gandhi, 23
The Garden of Earthly Delights, 16
Gardner, Robert, 108
Getino, Octavio, 84
Gibson, Evelyn, x–xi
Gimme Shelter, 55
Ginsburg, Faye, 58
  on ethics in ethnographic film, 116–17
The Gleaners and I (Les Glaneurs et la glaneuse), 45
Godard, Jean-Luc
  advocacy film group of, 82
  advocacy film influenced by, 86
  on cinema verité, 52
Godmilow, Jill, 24–25
Gold, Dan, 8
Goldenberg, Sonia, 76
The Good Fight, 100
Gore, Al, 7–8, 122
government funding, 18–20
government propaganda documentary
  advocacy film *v.*, 77–78
  Britain and, 66, 68–69, 72
  Canada and, 75
  effectiveness of, 71, 73–74
  ethics and, 74–75
  format of, 65
  Grierson, John, and, 67
  Japan and, 66, 71, 73–74, 75
  legacy of, 75–77
  Lorentz and, 67
  Nazi Germany and, 65–66, 68, 71
  public affairs documentary *v.*, 65
  Soviets and, 66
  United States and, 66–67, 70–71, 72–73
  Vertov and, 67
  World War I and, 65
Grass, 107
The Great Adventure, 119
Greene, Felix, 61
Greenfield, Lauren, 50
Greenwald, Robert, 21
Grierson, John, 3, 31, 127, 129–30, 132
  advocacy film influenced by, 86
  career beginnings of, 32–33
  on Challenge for Change, 49
  critical opinion on work of, 36–37
  first films of, 33–35
  on Flaherty, Robert, 35
  Flaherty, Robert, influence on, 33
  Flaherty, Robert, *v.*, 38
  Flaherty, Robert, working with, 34
  government propaganda documentary and, 67, 74–75
  influence of, 35–36

Grierson (*Cont.*)
  legacy of, 37–38
  on *Moana*, 33
  realism of, 25–26
  on social function of documentary, 35
  third cinema v., 84
  Vertov and influence on, 44
Grierson, Ruby, 33–34
Griffith, D.W., 27
Grizzly Man, 122
Guggenheim, Davis, 7–8, 122
Guynn, William, 133
Guzmán, Patricio
  The Battle of Chile and, 85
  Chile, Obstinate Memory and, 103–4
  Ivens and, 85

H

Hampton, Henry, x, 99, 128
Handsworth Songs, 101–2
Hansen, Jim, 8
Happy Mother's Day, 47
Hara, Kazuo, 99
Harlan County, U.S.A., 88
Hearts and Minds, 62
Helfand, Judith, 8
Helmrich, Leonard Retel, 108–9
Hemmingway, Ernest, 80
Hennebelle, Guy, 54
Herzog, Werner
  on cinema verité, 52
  Grizzly Man and, 122
Hiding and Seeking, 104
Hiroshima-Nagasaki, August 1945, 73–74
historical documentary
  biographies and, 95–97
  challenges facing, 91–92
  copyright issues facing, 94–95
  Holocaust and, 104
  personal films and, 100–105
  print historians v., 91–92
  responsibilities when making, 105–6
  revisionism and, 97–100
  stories and, 92–95
Hoberman, J., 129
Hollywood: The Golden Years, 94
Home for Life, 88
Honkasalo, Pirjo, x, 9
Hoop Dreams, 54, 54–55, 88
Horne, Lena, 83
Hôtel des Invalides, 46
Hour of the Furnaces (La Hora de los hornos), 84–85, 90–91
Housing Problems, 34
Houston, Bobby, 23
How the Myth Was Made, 31
Hudson, Robert, 23
The Hunters, 110
Hunting the White Bear, 118
Huston, John, 73

I

Ichikawa, Kon, 49
Images d'Ostende, 15
IMAX, 120–21
India 67, 49
Industrial Britain, 34
In Search of the Edge, 13
Inside North Vietnam, 61
interviews
  ethics of, 98–99
  Murrow and famous, 60–61
In the King of Prussia, 24
In the Land of the War Canoes, 28
In the Year of the Pig, 62
Into the Arms of Strangers, 100
Iraq for Sale, 90–91
Irwin, Steve, 119, 124
Isaacs, Jeremy, 97–98
Iskra group, 82
Ivens, Joris, 1, 15, 128
  advocacy film and, 79

on cinema verité, 52
Cuba filmmakers and, 83
Guzmán and, 85
legacy of, 80–81
Iwasaki, Akira, 73–74

J

Jabor, Arnaldo, 51
Jacobs, Lewis, 131
Jacobson, Harlan, 4
Jacquet, Luc, 121
James, Steve, 88, 90
Jarecki, Eugene, 7
Jaszi, Peter, 95
Jennings, Humphrey, 69, 72
Johnson, Martin, 118–19
Johnson, Osa, 118–19
Julien, Isaac, 101

K

Kartemquin Films, 88–90
Kaufman, Boris, 15
Kaufman, Mikhail, 40
Kaul, Mani, 17
Kearton, Cherry, 118
Kieslowski, Krzysztof, 86
Kildea, Gary, 114
King, Allan, 50, 128, 130
King Kong, 107
Kino-Pravda, 39
Kirkman, Larry, x
Klawans, Stuart, 129
Koenig, Wolf, 53
Kofman, Amy Ziering, 96–97
Kopple, Barbara, 88, 128
Koyaanisqatsi, 15

L

Land without Bread (Las Hurdes: Tierra sin Pan), 13
Lanzmann, Claude, 98–99

The Last Waltz, 135
Leach, Jerry, 114
Leacock, Richard, 46–47, 110, 130
legacy
of advocacy film, 87–91
of Flaherty, Robert, 32
of government propaganda documentary, 75–77
of Grierson, John, 37–38
of Ivens, 80–81
of Rouch, 112–13
of third cinema, 87–91
of Vertov, 43–44
of Wiseman, 50
Legacy of the Tundra, 116
Lewis, Chris, x
Lewis, Mark, 122
Leyda, Jay, 43
The Life and Times of Rosie the Riveter, 99
Linden, Adrienne, 110
Lippman, Walter, 33
Listen to Britain, 69
success of, 72–73
The Living Desert, 120
The Living Earth, 121
Loader, Jayne, 75
London Can Take It, 72
London Film-Makers Co-op, 82
London Women's Film Co-op, 82
Lonely Boy, 47
Lonelygirl15, 126–27
Longinotto, Kim, 45
Loose Change, 126
Lorentz, Pare, 6, 130
government propaganda documentary and, 67
Los Angeles Plays Itself, 15–16
Louisiana Story, 30
The Lovely May, 51
Lumumba: Death of a Prophet, 102

M

MacDougall, David
  approach to filmmaking of, 113
  on memory and film, 100
MacDougall, Judith, 113
Maclear, Michael, 61
The Mad Twenties, 94
Les Maîtres Fous, 111–12
Manhatta, 14
manipulation, reality *v.*, 2, 24–25
Man of Aran, 29–30
  myth of, 31
Man with a Movie Camera, 1, 15, *43*
  commentary of, 41–42
March of the Penguins, 6
  synopsis of, 121
Marker, Chris
  advocacy film group of, 82
  new techniques of, 51
  Sans Soleil and, 24
  Valparaiso, Mi Amor and, 85
Marshall, Herbert, 43
Marshall, John, 110
Marx, Leo, 30
Maysles, Albert, 46–47, 130, 132
  critical opinion on work of, 55
Maysles, David, 46–47, 130, 132
  critical opinion on work of, 55
McAllister, Stewart, 69
McKibben, Bill, 124
McLane, Betsy, 131
McNab, David, 23
Mekas, Jonas, 16
Michaels, Eric, 114
Michelson, Annette, 43
Middletown, 53–54
Mighty Times: Volume 2: The Children's March, 23
A Mighty Wind, 14
Minamata, 86
Mitmann, Gregg, 123
Moana, 3, 29, 33
mockumentary, 13–14
Moffat, Tracey, 116
Moi, un Noir, 112
Momma Don't Allow, 46
Mondo Cane, 107
Montagu, Ivor, 31
Moore, Michael, 4
  advocacy film *v.*, 78
  propaganda *v.*, 7
Morawski, Piotr, 76
Morin, Edgar, 51
Morley Safer's Vietnam, 61
Morris, Errol, 3–4
  approach to biography of, 97
  on cinema verité, 52
Mothlight, 16, *17*
Moyers, Bill, 59–60
Murrow, Edward R.
  on balance in film, 2
  corporate funding and, 20
  famous interviews by, 60–61
  personality of, 62

N

N!ai: The Story of a !Kung Woman, 110
Nanook of the North, 2, *29*, 107
  cultural impact of, 27–28
  making of, 27
  nobility in, 30
National Film Board (NFB). *See* Canadian National Film Board
Native Land, 81
Natural History of Chicken, 122
Nature, 120
nature documentary, 117
  beginnings of, 118–19
  blue chip and, 120
  environmental movement in, 121–23
  ethics and, 123–24
  IMAX and, 120–21
  Walt Disney studios and, 119–20
Navajo Film Project, 106–7
Nejvesti Prani, 51

Nelson, Joyce, on Grierson, John, 37
The New Americans, 88–90, *89*
NFB. *See* National Film Board
Nichols, Bill
  on documentary and postmodernism, 133
  ethics and, 22
  on personal documentaries, 105
  techniques of, 132
Nicht löschbares Feuer (The Indistinguishable Fire), 24
Night Mail, 34, 34–35
Nixon, Richard, 59
Nonfiction Film: A Critical History (Barsam), 131
Nornes, Markus, 134
Noujaim, Jehane, 125
Nova, 56
Now, 83
Nykino, 81

O

O Dreamland, 46
Ogawa, Shinsuke, 85–86
Oil on Ice, 90
One Sixth of the World, 42
Onwurah, Ngozi, 102
Ophuls, Marcel, 98
Opinião Publica (Public Opinion), 51
O'Rourke, Dennis, 114
Oshima, Nagisa, 49
Østergaard, Anders Høgsboro, 104–5
Our Wonderful World, 108
Outfoxed, 21

P

Padilha, José, 8–9
Panorama, 58
The Path to 9/11, 23
Patwardhan, Anand, 82

Peasants of the Second Fortress, 85
Peck, Raoul, 102
Pennebaker, D A, 46, 53, 110
Peralta, Stacy, 1
  Dogtown and Z-Boys and, 104
Perfumed Nightmare, 24
Perlmutter, Alvin, 59–60
Perrin, Jacques, 121
personal diary format, 8
Pilger, John, 64
The Plow that Broke the Plains, 6, 67
P.O.V., 60
The Power of Nightmares, 60–61
Primary, 47
propaganda, 6–7. *See also* government propaganda documentary
  Fahrenheit 9/11 v., 7
  Moore *v.,* 7
public affairs documentary
  cinema verité and, 63
  conventions of, 62–63
  critical opinion on work of, 63–64
  decline of, 58–59
  Drew and, 63
  ethics and, 63–64
  format of, 56–57
  government propaganda documentary *v.,* 65
  influence and significance of, 60–62
  journalists and, 57–58
  present state of, 64–65
  public television and, 59–60
  television and opportunities for, 58

Q

A Question of Equality, 99–100
Quinn, Gordon, x–xi, 88, 90

R

Rabiger, Michael, 3
Radio Bikini, 75
Rafferty, Kevin, 75
Rafferty, Pierce, 75
Rain, 1, 15
Rainer, Yvonne, 101
Raphael, Chad, 19
Rat, 122
realism, 26, 40, 133
reality
   artistry v., 25–26
   documentary and, 5, 9–12
   manipulation v., 2, 24–25
reenactment
   ethics of, 22–23
   history of, 22
Reeves, Nicholas, 71
Reggio, Godfrey, 15
Reiner, Rob, 13–14
Reisz, Karel, 46
Reith, John, 33
Rejger, Katarina, 126
Renov, Michael
   on personal documentary, 105
   techniques of, 132
Rich, Ruby, 129
Richter, Hans, 17
Riding Giants, 1
Riefenstahl, Leni, 68, 130
   Capra v., 70
   on government propaganda documentary, 75
Rien que les Heures, 15
The River, 6, 67
Roger and Me, 4
Rønde, Jeppe, 24
Roosevelt in Africa, 118
Roots, 23
Rosenbaum, Jonathan, 129
Rosteck, Thomas, 64
Rotha, Paul
   on documentary, 129
   on Flaherty, Robert, 31
   on Grierson, John, 36–37
Roth, Lorna, 114
Rouch, Jean, 128
   approach to filmmaking of, 111–13
   on cinema verité, 53
   direct cinema of, 52
   on documentary, 112
   Flaherty, Robert, influence on, 111
   legacy of, 112–13
   process of, 50–51
   Vertov influence on, 111
Rouquier, Georges, 119
Rubbo, Michael, 62
Ruby, Jay
   on ethnographic film, 106
   on Flaherty, Robert, 31–32
Rudavsky, Oren, 104
The Russian Miracle, 93
Ruttmann, Walther, 14–15

S

Sad Song of Yellow Skin, 62
Salesman, 47, *48*
Salomon, Henry "Pete," 93
Sankofa workshop, 101–2
Sans Soleil, 24
Schatz, Thomas, 135
Schlesinger, Arthur, 91
Schneeman, Carolee, 16
Schulberg, Budd, 74–75
Schwartzman, Stephan, xi
Scorsese, Martin, 44, 135
Sea Island, 119–20
Seavey, Nina, xi
The Secret Plot to Kill Hitler, 23
Secrets of Nature, 118
The Secret Tapes, 76
See It Now, 20, 58
   famous episodes of, 60
The Selling of the Pentagon, 61–62, 75
The Seoul Visual Collective, 87
Seven Up, 63

Shamir, Yo'av, 9
Shape of the Moon, 108–9
Sheeler, Charles, 14
Shoah, 98–99
Shub, Esfir, 92–93
Sierra Club, 90
Sierra Club Chronicles, 77
Simba, 118–19
Simma, Paul-Anders, 116
60 Minutes, 58–59, 64
Skorzewski, Edward, 86
Smith, Hedrick, 59–60
Snow, Michael, 16
Solanas, Fernando, 84
Song of Ceylon, 66
The Sorrow and the Pity, 98
The Spaghetti Story, 13
Spain, Tom, 58–59
The Spanish Earth, 90–91
   CP connection to, 80
   Flaherty, Robert, influence on, 80
   synopsis of, 80–81
Special Inquiry, 58
Spurlock, Morgan, 125
Star Wars, 1
Stone, Robert, 75
Stoney, George, xi
   advocacy film and, 87–88
   Flaherty, Robert influence on, 30–31
Stop Making Sense, 135
Storck, Henri, 15
   on *Borinage*, 79
The Story of the Weeping Camel, 32, 108
Strand, Paul, 14
Stranger with a Camera, 63–64
Sucksdorff, Arne, 119
Sukhdev, S., 49
Super Size Me, 125
Sussex, Elizabeth, 37
Sutton, Ron, x
Svilova, Elizaveta, 40
The Swenkas, 24
Symphony of the Don Basin, 42

T

Taboo, 108
Tahimik, Kidlat, 24
Tak for Alt, 22
Taking Pictures, 113
Tango of Slaves, 104
Teno, Jean-Marie, 102
Thin, 50
The Thin Blue Line, 3–4
third cinema
   Argentina and, 84–85
   Chile and, 85
   Cuba and, 83
   Grierson, John, v., 84
   Japan and, 85–86
   legacy of, 87–91
   Soviets and, 86
   Taiwan and, 86
This is Spinal Tap!, 13–14
Thorndike, Andrew, 93
Thorndike, Annelie, 93
Three Rooms of Melancholia, 9
Tie Xi Qu, 45
Tintin and I, 104–5
Tire Dié (Throw Me a Dime), 83, 86
Titicut Follies, 49–50
   Warrendale v., 50
Tokyo Olympiad, 49
Tomaselli, Keyan, 36
Triumph of the Will, 9, 72
   counterpropaganda from, 73
   political aims of, 68
   success of, 71
Trobriand Cricket, 114, 116
Tsuchimoto, Noriaki, 86
Twentieth Century, 58–59
20/20, 58
Two Laws, 116

U

Unik, Pierre, 13
Union Maids, 100
Untold Stories (Aufderheide and Jaszi), 95

V

Valparaiso, Mi Amor, 85
van den Broek, Eric, 126
van Dongen, Helen, 80
   on Flaherty, Robert, 31–32
The Vanishing Prairie, 120
Varda, Agnes, x, 45
Vaughan, Dai, x
Vertov, Dziga, 15, 25, 127, 130, 132
   advocacy film influenced by, 86
   on art *v.* realism, 40
   beliefs of, 38
   career beginnings of, 39–40
   career decline of, 42
   on communism and film, 39
   critical opinion on work of, 41
   on fiction *v.* documentary, 1, 38–39
   Flaherty, Robert, *v.*, 44
   government propaganda documentary and, 67
   Grierson, John, influenced by, 44
   legacy of, 43–44
   on love for camera, 14
   Rouch influenced by, 111
Victory at Sea, 76
   making of, 93
Video Diaries, 55
Video Letters project, 126
Vigo, Jean, 15
von Furstenberg, Diane, 96

W

Wal-Mart: The High Cost of Low Price, 6–7
Walt Disney studios, 119–20
Warrendale, 50
Watkins, Peter, 24
Watt, Harry, 34
Waves of Revolution, 82
The Wedding Camels: A Turkana Marriage, 113
Weisberg, Roger, 59–60
Wenguang, Wu, 87
West of Tracks, 45
What Farocki Thought, 24–25
White Paper, 58
Why We Fight, 7
   political aim of, 70–71
   success of, 73
Wild Man Blues, 88
Williams, Linda, 105
Winged Migration, 121
Winston, Brian
   on documentary, 133
   on Grierson, John, 37
Wintonick, Peter, 53
Wiseman, Fred, 110, 130
   career of, 49–50
   critical opinion on work of, 53
   on labeling his films, 52
   legacy of, 50
With Babies and Banners, 100
Wolf, Daniel, 96
Wolper, David, 94
The World at War, 97–98
World in Action, 58
Worth, Sol, 106–7
Wright, Basil, 34, 66

Y

You Are on Indian Land, 115

Z

Ziv, Ilan, 104
Zwerin, Charlotte, 47
Zwigoff, Terry, 55

Visit the
VERY SHORT INTRODUCTIONS
Web Site

www.oup.co.uk/vsi

- ▶ **Information** about all published titles
- ▶ News of **forthcoming books**
- ▶ **Extracts** from the books, including titles not yet published
- ▶ **Reviews** and views
- ▶ **Links** to other **web sites** and main OUP web page
- ▶ Information about **VSIs in translation**
- ▶ **Contact** the editors
- ▶ **Order** other **VSIs** on-line

Expand your collection of
VERY SHORT INTRODUCTIONS

1. Classics
2. Music
3. Buddhism
4. Literary Theory
5. Hinduism
6. Psychology
7. Islam
8. Politics
9. Theology
10. Archaeology
11. Judaism
12. Sociology
13. The Koran
14. The Bible
15. Social and Cultural Anthropology
16. History
17. Roman Britain
18. The Anglo-Saxon Age
19. Medieval Britain
20. The Tudors
21. Stuart Britain
22. Eighteenth-Century Britain
23. Nineteenth-Century Britain
24. Twentieth-Century Britain
25. Heidegger
26. Ancient Philosophy
27. Socrates
28. Marx
29. Logic
30. Descartes
31. Machiavelli
32. Aristotle
33. Hume
34. Nietzsche
35. Darwin
36. The European Union
37. Gandhi
38. Augustine
39. Intelligence
40. Jung
41. Buddha
42. Paul
43. Continental Philosophy
44. Galileo
45. Freud
46. Wittgenstein
47. Indian Philosophy
48. Rousseau
49. Hegel
50. Kant
51. Cosmology
52. Drugs
53. Russian Literature
54. The French Revolution
55. Philosophy
56. Barthes
57. Animal Rights
58. Kierkegaard

59. Russell
60. Shakespeare
61. Clausewitz
62. Schopenhauer
63. The Russian Revolution
64. Hobbes
65. World Music
66. Mathematics
67. Philosophy of Science
68. Cryptography
69. Quantum Theory
70. Spinoza
71. Choice Theory
72. Architecture
73. Poststructuralism
74. Postmodernism
75. Democracy
76. Empire
77. Fascism
78. Terrorism
79. Plato
80. Ethics
81. Emotion
82. Northern Ireland
83. Art Theory
84. Locke
85. Modern Ireland
86. Globalization
87. Cold War
88. The History of Astronomy
89. Schizophrenia
90. The Earth
91. Engels
92. British Politics
93. Linguistics
94. The Celts
95. Ideology
96. Prehistory
97. Political Philosophy
98. Postcolonialism
99. Atheism
100. Evolution
101. Molecules
102. Art History
103. Presocratic Philosophy
104. The Elements
105. Dada and Surrealism
106. Egyptian Myth
107. Christian Art
108. Capitalism
109. Particle Physics
110. Free Will
111. Myth
112. Ancient Egypt
113. Hieroglyphs
114. Medical Ethics
115. Kafka
116. Anarchism
117. Ancient Warfare
118. Global Warming
119. Christianity
120. Modern Art
121. Consciousness
122. Foucault
123. Spanish Civil War
124. The Marquis de Sade
125. Habermas
126. Socialism
127. Dreaming
128. Dinosaurs
129. Renaissance Art

130. Buddhist Ethics
131. Tragedy
132. Sikhism
133. The History of Time
134. Nationalism
135. The World Trade Organization
136. Design
137. The Vikings
138. Fossils
139. Journalism
140. The Crusades
141. Feminism
142. Human Evolution
143. The Dead Sea Scrolls
144. The Brain
145. Global Catastrophes
146. Contemporary Art
147. Philosophy of Law
148. The Renaissance
149. Anglicanism
150. The Roman Empire
151. Photography
152. Psychiatry
153. Existentialism
154. The First World War
155. Fundamentalism
156. Economics
157. International Migration
158. Newton
159. Chaos
160. African History
161. Racism
162. Kabbalah
163. Human Rights
164. International Relations
165. The American Presidency
166. The Great Depression and The New Deal
167. Classical Mythology
168. The New Testament as Literature
169. American Political Parties and Elections
170. Bestsellers
171. Geopolitics
172. Antisemitism
173. Game Theory
174. HIV/AIDS
175. Documentary Film

JOURNALISM
A Very Short Introduction
Ian Hargreaves

Journalism has an indelible effect on our worldview-from global terrorism to the American presidential elections, celebrity scandal to the latest environmental disaster. Here, renowned British journalist Ian Hargreaves uses his unique position within the media to examine how we get this information, and the practical, political, and professional decisions faced by journalists.

Is journalism the "first draft of history" or a dumbing-down of our culture and a glorification of the trivial and intrusive? In this intriguing book, Hargreaves presents a truly international perspective. Journalists, he says, should be more self-critical. But the core principles of press freedom and holding power to account are as vital today as they ever were.

> "Hargreaves has written a timely and disturbing account of journalism in peril."
>
> **Martin Bell, *The Times***

> "Ian Hargreaves is a distinguished journalist and academic with a fine track record of editorial integrity and incisive thought."
>
> **Chris Cramer, Managing Director, CNN International**

www.oup.co.uk/isbn/978-0-19-280656-7

PHOTOGRAPHY
A Very Short Introduction
Steve Edwards

Modern societies are saturated with photographs. From holiday snapshots to newspapers, advertisements, and the pristine walls of fine art galleries, photographs can be found everywhere, performing an extraordinary range of functions.

This Very Short Introduction looks at the ideas and concepts that underlie photography in its many incarnations. It asks what particular characteristics define a photograph, and how these characteristics affect the way we understand an image. Examining issues as varied as the claims for an "art of photography," the politics of observation, and the impact of digital photography, Steve Edwards provides a sense of the historical development of the medium alongside a clear account of many of the key critical issues.

www.oup.co.uk/isbn/978-0-19-280164-7